12—

Jack Russell

from

Aunt Frances & Aunt Bea

Private Houses
An International Survey

Werner Weidert

Private Houses

An International Survey

Frederick A. Praeger, Publishers
New York · Washington

BOOKS THAT MATTER

Published in the United States of America in 1967
by Frederick A. Praeger, Inc., Publishers
111 Fourth Avenue, New York, N.Y. 10003
All rights reserved
Copyright in Stuttgart in 1967 by Verlag Gerd Hatje, Stuttgart, Germany
Library of Congress Catalog Card Number: 67–29466
Translation into English: E. Rockwell
Printed in Germany

Contents · Inhalt

Introduction

Despite the rising costs of building construction and growing difficulties in obtaining suitable plots of land, the single-family house has not yet lost any of its attractions. The terrace house or the owner-occupied flat are still regarded by many as a reluctantly accepted compromise. This attitude has not been affected by the fact that some most attractive variations of these forms have been developed in recent years.

What are, in fact, the advantages of the single-family house? A well-planned owner-occupied house can provide an environment adapted to the owner's personal way of life, unrestricted by considerations for other people living in the building or in the immediate neighbourhood. Unlike a rented flat, an owner-occupied house offers the maximum of freedom and the garden, which is nearly always attached, can itself provide an extension of the living space. Just how important this living within and with the landscape has become is proved by numerous examples in the present book.

Building sites are scarce and expensive, particularly in the bigger cities and in reasonably accessible districts. For this reason, sites are being developed which, even twenty years ago, would have been considered unsuitable for the purpose. Steeply sloping ground, exposed positions, rocky or marshy subsoils all give rise to a number of difficulties; however, these are seldom insuperable and may, on the contrary, often be turned to advantage. A steep slope, for example, need not involve costly excavation works – by stepping the building down the slope, both upper and lower floors can be given access at ground level, and the raised living room will offer a wider view. Where the water table is high, the house can be set on stilts. The open ground floor is useful as a covered play space for children or as a car port, saving the cost of a garage. Even the difficulties of rocky ground can be overcome without expensive blasting operations, by the imaginative use of stanchions, and difficult access to sites on mountain slopes counterbalanced by the advantages derived from the fine views and complete privacy. On a narrow plot, screen walls flanking the living room will achieve the necessary degree of seclusion. Where houses are arranged in groups, it is still possible to comply with the client's personal requirements by varying their orientation and plan. Where the distance from neighbours and the size of the plot allow, architects and builders nearly always make use of this great advantage of the wholly detached house by opening it up to its surroundings. There are, however, instances where the architect has deliberately preferred to forego such outward orientation. A case in point is the house of the Danish architect Knud Friis (page 74) where the landscape is deliberately shut out despite the fact that a major part of the plot thus remains unexploited. He has chosen, on the ground floor, the privacy of a fully enclosed patio rather than the open vista; this is reserved as an unexpected pleasure for the living rooms on the upper floor.

A similar attitude, emphasizing the protective function of the house, is displayed by H. Taylor's house (page 162) which, perhaps significantly, is also constructed in concrete. If, in this case, intercommunication with the natural surroundings has been almost completely

1. On rocky sites, the necessary level ground is produced by employing retaining walls. (Page 94)

1. Auf den Felsen schaffen Stützmauern den benötigten ebenen Baugrund. (Seite 94)

2. The living room floor is raised on stilts above the lake-side reeds. The open ground floor serves as a car port. (Page 84)

2. Stützen heben das Wohngeschoß über das Uferschilf. Das offene Erdgeschoß dient als Wageneinstellplatz. (Seite 84)

3. Interior and exterior merge. (Page 12)

3. Innen- und Außenraum fließen ineinander. (Seite 12)

4. The entire living room area is screened by high redwood panels. (Page 64)
5. Fireside area, sitting room and dining area are combined in a single, large room. (Page 154)

4. Hohe Rotholzpanels schirmen die gesamte Wohnfläche ab. (Seite 64)
5. Kaminplatz, Sitzbereich und Eßplatz sind zu einem großen vielgestaltigen Raum vereinigt. (Seite 154)

renounced, an outstanding example of the opposite approach is provided by Franzen's house (page 158) where the living room has become a merely glass-protected part of the site. With the exception of the bedrooms, the house is completely open and is defined visually merely by the protecting roof and the floor slab.

These two extremes mark the wide scale of possible treatment, ranging from houses on simple square or rectangular plans through L-shaped, T-shaped or cruciform plans to the patio house built around a central courtyard or garden.

Personal predilections for certain forms of lay-out, e. g. with open plan or juxtaposed cells, specific space requirements depending on the size and composition of the family and, last but not least, the handwriting of the architect, confer on a well-designed single-family house a character of unmistakable individuality. But such individuality is due only to different combinations of the same elementary functions: sleeping, eating, working, relaxing and playing. Although these basic functions may be related in a great variety of different ways, the means of serving them are, in most cases, the same. The lay-out is frequently based on the open plan, which is, however, in most cases confined to the living areas. In nearly all cases, living room and dining room are combined. Sometimes, this general area may also include a place for a desk serving as study, or more rarely the hall and/or kitchen. Among the devices used for separating the different sub-areas are pieces of furniture and storage units, the fireplace, movable partitions, sliding doors and split-level arrangements.

A family is not a static unit, but one undergoing continual change. For a house to meet the ever-changing requirements of a family which will first grow and then shrink, its lay-out must be flexible, allowing from the outset for the possibility of extension by providing rooms which are not in continuous use or are not assigned to any specific purpose. Flexibility can also be aided by opening the children's bedrooms on to a playroom-type hall, or by

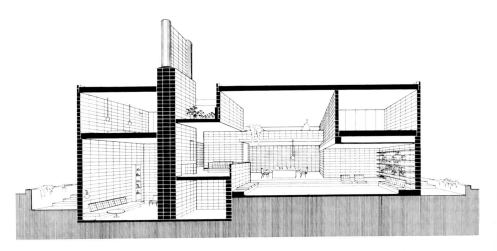

8

6. The open plan can be modified by sliding doors. (Page 24)

6. Der Raumfluß kann durch Schiebetüren unterbrochen werden. (Seite 24)

7. The ground floor is used by the whole family, the first floor is reserved for the children; on the second floor is the master bedroom. (Page 148)

7. Das Erdgeschoß wird von der ganzen Familie benutzt, das erste Obergeschoß ist den Kindern vorbehalten und im zweiten Obergeschoß befindet sich der Elternschlafraum. (Seite 148)

including multi-purpose rooms which may for instance serve either as guest room or as study. Open planning and flexibility can be most easily obtained by resorting to framework construction with nonstructural partitions allowing for an adaptation to changing requirements. The living room is usually the focus of daily family life and its orientation is always governed by the desire to enjoy as much sunshine and as much of a beautiful view as possible. It often includes an open fireplace, frequently incorporating a low-level fireside seat. Large windows, often occupying an entire wall, enable daylight and sunshine to penetrate far into the room.

It is the open contact with the landscape, even more than the flat roof, which must be regarded as the most significant characteristic of the modern house. Large windows make the natural surroundings part of the interior. Flower beds, the same level inside and outside the windows, dissolve the boundary between interior and exterior. Balconies and loggias serve as outdoor sitting-rooms. Terraces merging with the garden add a 'green room' to the interior spaces. Recesses or projections of the façade and cantilevered floor slabs create protected outdoor spaces, often adjoining a large lawn or a swimming pool. One drawback of large windows, the undesirable heating-up of the interior by solar heat, can be easily avoided by a sensible arrangement of plants or sun screening devices.

The sleeping quarters, calling for special privacy and protection, are preferably placed in a separate wing or storey. The master bedroom is nearly always the largest and is generally combined with a dressing room and a bathroom, often forming a self-contained suite within the main sleeping area.

The children are sometimes assigned to a self-contained area, with their own bedrooms and play rooms which, to minimize mutual disturbance, are placed in a special wing or, in many cases, on an upper or lower floor. Parents and children can thus remain in their separate parts of the house as they choose. The common forum is the living room or an additional room specially designed for this purpose, such as the television room.

The widest choice of location applies to the kitchen. Its exact position depends on whether there are children and how many there are in the family and whether or not domestic help is available to the housewife. Where resident staff is available, the well-tried lay-out of a self-contained staff wing with kitchen, utility room and maid's room, accessible from a separate entrance, is still resorted to. Where household help is not available, the housewife's activities are centred on the kitchen, in which case the kitchen is most usefully placed in the centre of the house to serve as a 'control room'. In this way, the housewife's walking distances are minimized and supervision of children is made easier. Such a kitchen will be linked with the dining area and often directly with the sitting room as well by a hatch which may also be used as a breakfast bar.

The garage or car port is an indispensable adjunct to a modern house. Advances in domestic technology have largely made cellars and storerooms unnecessary and the space they occupied is often taken by a hobby room or an additional nursery.

With the great range of building materials available, there is, so far as the single-family house is concerned, no longer any marked preference for specific materials chosen on grounds of regional tradition or special climatic conditions. There is, however, a marked tendency to leave the materials in their natural state, not only externally but also inside the house. This applies in particular to those materials which, because of their structural capabilities or surface texture, can be used to obtain certain aesthetic effects. But the use of such materials is generally confined to the living areas; the walls and ceilings of kitchen, children's rooms and bedrooms, being more purpose-governed, are still mainly plastered. Timber-clad ceilings and walls, exposed concrete and laminated wood beams, precast concrete blocks left unplastered, or concrete walls still showing the marks of the shuttering, are all common features. Interesting effects are often obtained from combinations of materials, particularly concrete and wood. Rubble walls, too, are used to provide a specific accent. There is, however, always a danger that such effects may be used for their own sake, and so detract from the unobtrusive yet individual background the living areas should provide for all the activities and objects they house.

In selecting these houses, the aim has been to present typical examples which illustrate the current trends and potentialities in house design. The order of presentation of the schemes is governed by the shape and size of the plan, beginning with the simple and comparatively small house with a rectangular plan. Specific features and special problems are discussed in the individual descriptions. It is hoped that a close study of these, together with the plans and photographs, will enable the reader to visualize what it would be like to live in these houses and so derive ideas and inspiration for his own building projects.

8. From the centrally placed kitchen, all the rooms are easily accessible. (Page 140)
9. Movable blinds afford protection against the sun. (Page 114)
10. The kitchen is completely integrated with the living room (Page 114)

8. Von der zentral gelegenen Küche lassen sich alle Räume auf kurzen Wegen erreichen. (Seite 140)
9. Bewegliche Lamellenroste schützen gegen die Sonne. (Seite 114)
10. Die Küche ist in den Wohnbereich einbezogen. (Seite 114)

Einleitung

Trotz steigender Baukosten und wachsender Schwierigkeiten bei der Grundstücksbeschaffung hat das Einfamilienhaus bis heute nichts von seiner Anziehungskraft eingebüßt. Das Reihenhaus oder die Eigentumswohnung im Mehrfamilienhaus werden von vielen als Kompromiß empfunden, den man ungern in Kauf nimmt. Daran ändert auch die Tatsache nichts, daß es auf diesem Gebiet inzwischen durchaus akzeptable Lösungen gibt.

Was sind nun die Vorteile des Einfamilienhauses? Bei durchdachter Planung kann man sich mit dem eigenen Haus einen dem persönlichen Lebensstil adäquaten Rahmen schaffen, in dem man weder auf andere Hausbewohner noch auf eine allzu enge Nachbarschaft Rücksicht nehmen muß. Als selbstgewähltes, nicht wie bei der Mietwohnung vorgefundenes »Gehäuse« bietet es ein Maximum an Bewegungsspielraum und durch den Garten, der fast immer zum Haus gehört, eine Erweiterung des Wohnbereichs. Wie wichtig man dieses Leben in und mit der Landschaft nimmt, beweisen viele Beispiele dieses Buches.

Grundstücke sind knapp und teuer, zumindest in den Ballungszentren und in einigermaßen verkehrsgünstiger Lage. Deshalb wird heute auch Gelände erschlossen, das noch vor zwanzig Jahren als unbebaubar galt. Stark abfallende Grundstücke, ausgesetzte Lage, felsiger oder nasser Baugrund bringen eine Reihe von Schwierigkeiten mit sich, die jedoch in keinem Falle unüberwindlich sind, ja im Gegenteil sich oft in Vorteile ummünzen lassen. So erspart der stark abfallende Hang kostspielige Ausschachtungsarbeiten; es ergeben sich ebenerdige Zugänge zu Unter- und Obergeschoß und aus dem angehobenen Wohngeschoß bietet sich freiere Aussicht. Bei hohem Grundwasserspiegel läßt sich das Haus auf Stützen stellen. Das offene Erdgeschoß ist willkommen als geschützter Kinderspielplatz oder als Einstellplatz für das Auto, der die Garage erspart. Auch Felsgrund läßt sich durch Stützen ohne teure Sprengungen bewältigen. Den Nachteil eines schwer zugänglichen Geländes an der Bergflanke wiegen die schöne Aussicht und die völlige Ungestörtheit auf. In der schmalen und tiefen Baulücke gewährleisten Schirmwände, zwischen denen der Wohnbereich liegt, das gewünschte Maß an Ungestörtheit. Zwei nebeneinander liegende Grundstücke können mit einem Doppelhaus überbaut werden, wobei jede Hälfte im Innern trotz äußerer Einheitlichkeit ihren individuellen Charakter bewahrt. Bei der Gruppierung mehrerer Einfamilienhäuser geben unter anderem Orientierung und Varianten der Grundrißgliederung die Möglichkeit, verschiedenen Ansprüchen gerecht zu werden.

Soweit es der Abstand zum Nachbarn und die Größe des Grundstücks erlauben, nützen Architekten und Bauherrn fast immer die bevorzugte Lage des allseitig frei stehenden Wohnhauses, indem sie es nach außen öffnen. Es gibt aber auch Fälle, in denen aus freien Stücken auf die Orientierung zum Außenraum hin verzichtet wird. So schließt beispielsweise der dänische Architekt Friis (Seite 74) sein Heim gegen die Außenwelt ab, obwohl dabei ein Großteil des Grundstücks ungenutzt bleibt. Er zieht die Intimität eines allseits umbauten Innenhofes dem offenen Ausblick vor, den er sich als Überraschungsmoment für die im Obergeschoß liegenden Wohnräume vorbehält.

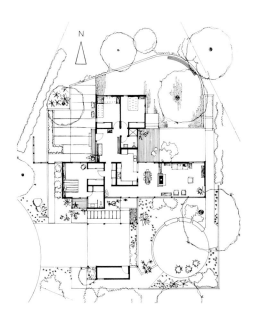

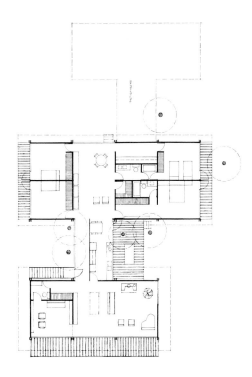

Eine ähnliche Auffassung, bei der die Funktion des Hauses als bergende Hülle betont wird, zeigt sich beim Haus Taylor (Seite 162), das interessanterweise ebenfalls aus Beton errichtet wurde. Ist hier auf die Öffnung zum Außenraum fast vollkommen verzichtet, so wird dagegen im Haus Franzen (Seite 158) der Wohnbereich zu einem in Glas gehüllten Teil des Grundstücks. Mit Ausnahme des Schlaftraktes ist das Haus völlig offen und wird optisch nur durch das schirmende Dach und die Bodenplatte umschrieben.

Diese beiden Extreme markieren die ganze Skala der Gestaltungsmöglichkeiten, angefangen vom Haus auf quadratischem oder rechteckigem Grundriß über winkelförmige, T-förmige und kreuzförmige Anlagen bis hin zum Atriumhaus, das um den Grünraum herum gebaut wird.

Individuelle Wohnvorstellungen – etwa vom Ineinanderfließen offener Raumteile oder von der Addition in sich geschlossener Zellen –, der von der Familiengröße und -zusammensetzung abhängige Raumbedarf und nicht zuletzt die Handschrift des Architekten machen das gute Einfamilienhaus zu einem unverwechselbaren Gebilde. Diese Einmaligkeit resultiert jedoch aus einer Kombination gleichbleibender Funktionselemente wie Schlafen, Essen, Arbeiten, Wohnen und Spielen. Diese Grundelemente des Wohnvorganges können zwar variiert und unterschiedlich zusammengesetzt werden, die Mittel zu ihrer Bewältigung sind jedoch in vielen Fällen die gleichen.

Ausgangspunkt für die Grundrißdisposition ist häufig die Idee vom Raumfluß, die jedoch fast immer nur auf den Wohnbereich angewendet wird. In nahezu allen Fällen sind Wohnraum und Eßzimmer zu einem Raum vereinigt. Einbezogen werden kann das Studio in Form eines Arbeitsplatzes, seltener die Diele und die Küche. Möbel, der Kaminblock, bewegliche Wände, Schiebetüren und Geschoßversetzung sind die Mittel, deren man sich zur Trennung der verschiedenen Bereiche untereinander bedient.

Der Schlafbereich wird als Zone eines besonders schutzbedürftigen und intimen Wohnvorganges gern in einem eigenen Trakt oder Geschoß untergebracht. Regelmäßig am größten ist der Elternschlafraum, dem meist ein Ankleideraum und ein Bad zugeordnet sind. Elternschlafraum, Ankleideraum und Bad können eine eigene Raumgruppe innerhalb des Schlafbereiches bilden, der eine Gruppe von Kinder- oder Gästezimmern gegenübersteht.

Die größten Variationsmöglichkeiten für die Einfügung in den Gesamtgrundriß ergeben sich bei der Küche. Wie man sie einordnet, hängt davon ab, ob und wie viele Kinder zum Haushalt gehören und ob die Hausfrau eine Hilfe hat. In Häusern mit Personal gibt es immer noch die bewährte Einrichtung eines Personalflügels mit Küche, Hauswirtschaftsraum und Mädchenzimmer, von außen zugänglich über einen Separateingang. Fehlen Hilfskräfte, dann rückt das Reich der Hausfrau bildlich und praktisch in den Mittelpunkt. Die Küche wird dann gern, um der Hausfrau die Wege zu verkürzen und um ihr die Beaufsichtigung der Kinder zu erleichtern, als zentrale »Schaltstelle« in die Mitte gelegt und über eine Durchreiche, die zugleich als Frühstücksbar dienen kann, mit dem Eßplatz oder unmittelbar mit dem Wohnraum verbunden.

11. A third wing can be added without the need for major structural alterations. (Page 124)
12, 13. Adjacent to the living room is the outdoor lounge. (Pages 158 and 20)

11. Ein dritter Flügel läßt sich anfügen, ohne daß wesentliche Änderungen am baulichen Bestand vorgenommen werden müssen. (Seite 124)
12, 13. An den Wohnraum schließt sich das grüne Zimmer an. (Seiten 158 und 20)

Page / Seite 11:

14–16. Stone and wood are sympathetically related. (Pages 40, 90 and 51)

14–16. Stein und Holz sind harmonisch miteinander verbunden. (Seiten 40, 90 und 51)

Der hohe Stand der Haustechnik erlaubt einen weitgehenden Verzicht auf Keller- und Vorratsräume. An ihre Stelle tritt häufig ein Hobbyraum oder ein zusätzliches Kinderspielzimmer. Eine Selbstverständlichkeit für das Einfamilienhaus ist heute die Garage oder der Autoeinstellplatz.

Die Familie ist keine statische, sondern eine sich stets wandelnde Gemeinschaft. Um ihrem Wachsen und Schrumpfen und ihren sich immer wieder ändernden Bedürfnissen gerecht zu werden, sollte das Haus eine gewisse Flexibilität gewährleisten. Sie läßt sich erreichen durch eine bereits in der Grundrißdisposition berücksichtigte Erweiterungsmöglichkeit und durch das Angebot von Räumen, die nicht ständig benutzt werden oder deren Verwendung nicht von vornherein festliegt. Auch die Einrichtung eines Spielflures vor dem Kinderzimmer oder die Möglichkeit, einen Raum für mehrere Zwecke, etwa als Kinder- oder Gästezimmer zu verwenden, tragen zur Flexibilität bei. Konstruktiv gibt der Einbau von nichttragenden Raumtrennwänden jederzeit die Möglichkeit, sich – wenn auch mit einigem Aufwand – an gewandelte Raumforderungen anzupassen. Raumfluß und Flexibilität lassen sich am einfachsten mit Skelettkonstruktionen erreichen.

Das Zentrum des täglichen Lebens bildet der Wohnraum. Von der Grundfläche her der größte Raum, wird er immer so orientiert, daß er die meiste Sonne bekommt oder die schönste Aussicht bietet. Zu seiner Ausstattung gehört vielfach der offene Kamin, häufig noch ergänzt durch den vertieft angelegten Kaminsitzplatz. Große, oft wandfüllende oder geschoßhohe Fenster stellen den Kontakt zur Außenwelt her und lassen Licht und Sonne weit in den Raum dringen.

Den Kindern wird sehr häufig ein eigener Bereich, bestehend aus Schlaf-Arbeitsräumen und Kinderspielzimmer zugewiesen, der im Interesse geringster gegenseitiger Störungen meist in einem besonderen Flügel, oft auch im Unter- oder Obergeschoß liegt. Das Leben von Eltern und Kindern kann so nach Wunsch in getrennten Bereichen verlaufen. Gemeinsamer Treffpunkt ist der Wohnraum oder ein eigens dafür bestimmter zusätzlicher Raum wie das Fernsehzimmer.

Weit mehr als das flache Dach kennzeichnet die Öffnung zur Natur das heutige Einfamilienhaus. Große Fenster beziehen die Umwelt optisch in den Innenraum ein. Niveaugleiche Pflanzenbecken vor und hinter der Fensterwand lassen die Grenze zwischen dem Drinnen und Draußen verfließen. Balkone und Loggien gestatten das Wohnen im Freien. Terrassen, die in den Garten übergehen, erweitern den Innenraum um das grüne Zimmer. Fassadenrücksprünge, ausgreifende Hausflügel und vorkragende Geschosse schaffen geschützte Freiräume, an die sich häufig große Rasenflächen mit Schwimmbecken anschließen. Die Nachteile der großen Fensterfronten, wie die unerwünschte Aufheizung der Innenräume durch Sonneneinstrahlung, kann man durch geschickte Bepflanzung oder Sonnenschutzvorrichtungen vermeiden.

Bei dem vielfältigen Angebot von Baustoffen läßt sich für das Einfamilienhaus keine Bevorzugung bestimmter Materialien erkennen, die durch nationale Vorliebe oder durch das spezifische Klima bedingt wäre. Auffallend ist jedoch das Bestreben, die verwendeten Materialien in ihrem natürlichen Zustand zu belassen, und zwar nicht nur außen, sondern auch im Innenraum. Das gilt insbesondere für die Baustoffe, mit denen sich auf Grund ihrer Struktur oder Oberflächenbeschaffenheit bestimmte Raumwirkungen erreichen lassen. Anwendung finden sie im allgemeinen nur im Wohnbereich, während Küche, Kinder- und Schlafzimmer als mehr zweckbestimmte Räume meist den traditionellen Verputz erhalten. So finden sich besonders häufig holzverschalte Decken oder Wände, sichtbar belassene Deckenunterzüge aus Beton oder Schichtholzbalken, unverputzte Betonformsteine oder schalungsrauher Beton als Wand. Interessante Wirkungen lassen sich in der Kombination, besonders von Beton und Holz, erzielen. Auch Natursteinmauern setzen einen spezifischen Akzent. Es besteht allerdings die Gefahr, daß derartige Effekte zum Selbstzweck werden und der Wohnraum jenes Mindestmaß an Neutralität verliert, das seine individuelle Ausstattung zuläßt.

Die Auswahl bemühte sich um die Zusammenstellung typischer Beispiele für die Tendenzen und Möglichkeiten im Einfamilienhausbau unserer Tage. Auf Besonderheiten und spezielle Probleme wird bei der Dokumentation des betreffenden Hauses, soweit sie sich daran zeigen, näher eingegangen. Die Gruppierung erfolgte nach Grundrißform und Größe, beginnend mit dem einfachen und verhältnismäßig kleinen Haus auf rechteckigem Grundriß. Eine eingehende Beschäftigung mit dem dargebotenen Material und der Versuch, sich selbst als Bewohner dieser Häuser zu sehen, wird dem Leser eine Reihe von Anregungen geben können.

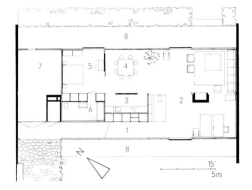

Architect's house near Rungsted, Denmark
Architect: Halldor Gunnlögsson

The plot, covering approx. 1700 sq. yards, adjoins the Sound between Copenhagen and Elsinore and falls from west to east by approx. 20 ft. The bungalow, designed for two persons, is placed across the slope and, being 66 ft. long, covers nearly the whole width of the plot. The two long sides are mainly glazed. Side walls and roof are projected on either side, thus creating covered and protected terraces on both long sides. The plan is based on a 1 metre module and is divided into ten-squares with sides of 4 metres length by the posts supporting the roof beams. Five of these squares are assigned to the living room and dining area in the southern part of the house, two to the garage with workshop, and one to the bedroom. The two remaining squares are taken up by kitchen, bathroom, entrance and hall. Boiler room, bathroom and kitchen are combined in a central core which is top lit. Bedroom and kitchen are separated from the adjacent dining area by sliding doors. Porch and hall are on the west side. Construction: Wooden posts on concrete foundations between two cross walls of white-plastered brick. Flat roof resting on three longitudinal beams of laminated wood. The ceiling panels between the roof rafters, which remain visible, consist of untreated deal battens. Flooring of grey Swedish marble. Underfloor heating.

1. View from the east. The night photograph clearly shows the generous way in which the space has been divided. On the left is the living room, merging with the dining room (centre); on the right, behind the sliding door, is the bedroom.
2. West front of the house, seen from the garden which is about 7 ft. higher. On the left, behind the trellis wall which ensures privacy, is the drive leading to the house. The entrance is screened by a lattice grille.
3. Plan. Key: 1 entrance and hall, 2 living room, 3 kitchen, 4 dining room, 5 bedroom, 6 bathroom and W.C., 7 garage and workshop, 8 terrace.
4. Section. The building is protected against overlooking from the road by the staggered levels and evergreen hedges.
5. The architect describes the basic idea of the design as follows: 'The house is intended to convey the impression of living on a covered terrace which, as it were, separates the secluded small and peaceful garden from the exciting and continuously changing spectacle of the sea.'

Architektenhaus bei Rungsted, Dänemark
Architekt: Halldor Gunnlögsson

Das annähernd 1400 Quadratmeter große Grundstück liegt an der Ostseeküste zwischen Kopenhagen und Helsingör. Es fällt von Westen nach Osten um rund 6 m. Das eingeschossige, für zwei Personen entworfene Haus, das quer zur Hangneigung steht, reicht mit 20 m Fassadenlänge fast über die ganze Breite. Die beiden Längsfronten sind weitgehend in Glas aufgelöst und gegenüber den Mauerscheiben auf den Stirnseiten zurückgesetzt, so daß sich davor jeweils eine überdachte Terrasse ergibt. Der Grundriß ist auf einem Rastermaß von 1 m aufgebaut. Durch die Ständer, die die Deckenbalken tragen, wird er in 10 Quadrate mit einer Seitenlänge von je 4 m aufgeteilt. Fünf dieser Quadrate entfallen auf Wohnraum mit Eßplatz in der Südhälfte des Hauses, zwei auf Garage mit Werkstatt und eines auf den Schlafraum. Die beiden restlichen sind auf Küche, Bad, Eingang und Diele verteilt. Heizraum, Bad und Küche wurden zu einem innenliegenden Naßkern zusammengefaßt, der über Oberlichter Tageslicht erhält. Schlafraum und Küche sind durch Schiebetüren vom angrenzenden Eßplatz getrennt. Windfang und Diele liegen auf der Westseite. Konstruktion: Holzständer auf Betonfundament zwischen zwei Quermauern aus weiß verputzten Ziegeln. Flachdach in Holzkonstruktion auf drei längsgespannten Schichtholzbalken. Bodenbelag grauer schwedischer Marmor. Die Deckenfelder zwischen den sichtbar belassenen Dachsparren sind mit Fichtenriemen verschalt. Fußbodenheizung.

1. Ostansicht. Die Nachtaufnahme läßt deutlich die großzügige Raumgliederung erkennen. Links der Wohnraum, der in den Eßraum (Mitte) übergeht, und rechts, hinter der Schiebetür, der Schlafraum.
2. Blick aus dem 2 m höher liegenden Garten auf die Westfront des Hauses. Links hinter der geflochtenen Sichtschutzwand die Zufahrt, von der aus man ins Haus gelangt. Vor dem Eingangsbereich ein screenartiger Lattenrost.
3. Grundriß. Legende: 1 Eingang und Diele, 2 Wohnraum, 3 Küche, 4 Eßzimmer, 5 Schlafraum, 6 Bad und WC, 7 Garage und Werkstatt, 8 Terrasse.
4. Gebäudeschnitt. Sichtschutz gegen die Straße durch Niveauversetzung und Hecken.
5. Der Architekt umschreibt die Grundidee der Planung mit den Worten: »Das Haus soll das Gefühl vermitteln, auf einer überdeckten Terrasse zu wohnen, die – sozusagen – den umfriedeten kleinen und stillen Garten vom erregenden, ständig wechselnden Schauspiel der See trennt.«

6. The architect's desk in the south-east corner of the living room. The brick end wall is faced with black-varnished wood. Desk and chair designed by Poul Kjaerholm.

7. Chairs, table and built-in bench in the living room. On the right the free-standing open fireplace, built up from white-plastered brick. Placed in the centre of the room, the fireplace serves to divide it. The effect of the different materials – wood for walls and ceilings, marble for the floor – is enhanced by the sparse furnishing.

8. Dining area, with partly open sliding door leading to the bedroom. Behind the closed sliding door on the left is the kitchen. The book-shelves are built-in. Three of the glazed panels visible in the picture are fixed, the fourth is designed as a sliding door. The windows have no curtains but can be screened by wooden shutters.

9. Sitting area, seen from the architect's working desk. The sea appears to be flooding right into the room.

6. Blick auf den Arbeitsplatz in der Südostecke des Wohnraums. Vor der gemauerten Stirnwand schwarz lackierte Holzschalung. Schreibtisch und Stuhl wurden von Poul Kjaerholm entworfen.

7. Die Sitzgruppe des Wohnraumes mit der eingebauten Sitzbank. Rechts der frei stehende, offene Kamin, aus weiß verputzten Ziegeln gemauert. In die Mitte des Raumes gestellt, dient er als Raumteiler. Die sparsame Möblierung bringt die verwendeten Materialien – Holz für Wände und Decken, Marmor für den Fußboden – besonders zur Geltung.

8. Blick auf den Eßplatz mit teilweise geöffneter Schiebetür zum Schlafraum. Hinter der geschlossenen Schiebetür links liegt die Küche. Die Regalwand ist eingebaut. Drei der auf dem Bild sichtbaren, raumhohen Fensterfelder sind fest verglast, das vierte ist als Glasschiebetür ausgebildet. Die Fenster haben keine Vorhänge, sie lassen sich durch Rollos aus Holzleistchen abschirmen.

9. Blick vom Arbeitsplatz auf die Sitzgruppe des Wohnraums. Das Meer scheint bis ins Zimmer zu fluten.

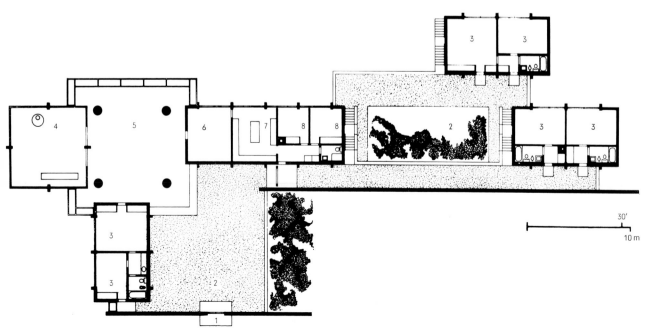

Boisonnas House at Cap Bénat, Côte d'Azur
Architect: Philip Johnson

The outstanding feature of this house is the unique beauty of its position, surrounded by pinewoods, and set high above the sea on the brow of a hill dominating the entire coast line and offering a wide panorama towards south and east. It consists of five self-contained dwelling units and serves mainly as a holiday home for a large family, although it is equipped with all the appliances required for permanent residence. The design has exploited the entire site. To a much greater extent than usual, the outdoor areas have become integrated with the internal ones. The boundaries between different areas are defined not by walls or ceilings but by the floors. On the north side, the living room is screened by two rubble walls. The centre of the complex is the covered patio which serves to link the central part, the living room and one of the dwelling units. The shell roof of the patio, composed of hyperparabolic panels, is supported by four sturdy tapering columns. The dwelling units all have a projecting reinforced concrete framework with non-structural panels which are plastered at ground floor level.

Haus Boisonnas am Cap Bénat, Côte d'Azur
Architekt: Philip Johnson

Einmalig schön ist die Lage dieses von Pinien umgebenen Hauses, das hoch über dem Meer auf einer die ganze Küste beherrschenden Bergkuppe steht, von der aus man nach Süden und Osten einen weiten Ausblick genießt. Der aus fünf Einzelbauten bestehende Komplex ist nicht ständig bewohnt. Er dient der vielköpfigen Familie vorzugsweise für länger dauernde Ferienaufenthalte, ist aber darüber hinaus mit allen Einrichtungen für ein ständiges Wohnen versehen. Die Planung des Architekten macht das ganze Grundstück zum Wohnbereich. Alle Freisitzplätze sind in einem über den Normalfall hinausgehenden Maße integrierter Bestandteil der Wohnfläche. Die Raumgrenzen ergeben sich nicht durch Wände und Decken, sie werden durch den Fußboden umschrieben. Zwei Natursteinmauern schirmen den Wohnbereich gegen Norden ab. Mittelpunkt der Anlage ist der überdachte Wohnhof, der den Zentralbau, den Wohnraum und einen Apartmentbau zu einer Einheit verbindet. Die aus hyperparabolischen Elementen zusammengefügte Dachschale des Wohnhofes ruht auf vier kräftigen konischen Stützen. Alle Gebäude sind ausgefachte Stahlbeton-Skelettkonstruktionen, deren Wandfelder zwischen den außenliegenden Stützen im Erdgeschoßbereich verputzt wurden.

1. Covered patio. Even the furniture (bought in consultation with the architect) reveals the character of this area as an outdoor lounge. On the left is the completely glazed living room which presents a wide panorama.
2. Plan. Key: 1 entrance, 2 solarium, 3 dwelling unit, 4 living room, 5 patio, 6 dining room, 7 kitchen, 8 staff.
3. Site plan.
4. The glass walls of the living room are designed as sliding doors. Living room and patio can be combined into a single unit, flooded with light and air. The unity is emphasized by using the same flooring of black slate flags in both. The dominating feature of the living room is the black iron fireplace which, in its cylindrical treatment, echoes the motif of the patio columns.

1. Blick in den überdachten Wohnhof. Schon das Mobiliar, bei dessen Kauf der Architekt beratend mitwirkte, läßt die Wertung dieser Freifläche als Innenraum erkennen. Links der rundum verglaste Wohnraum, aus dem man eine weite Aussicht hat.
2. Grundriß. Legende: 1 Eingang, 2 Sonnenhof, 3 Apartment, 4 Wohnraum, 5 Wohnhof, 6 Eßzimmer, 7 Küche, 8 Personal.
3. Lageplan.
4. Die Glaswände des Wohnraumes sind als Schiebetüren ausgebildet. Wohnraum und Wohnhof können zu einer licht- und luftdurchfluteten Einheit verbunden werden. Diesen Eindruck der Zusammengehörigkeit verstärkt der in beiden Räumen gleiche Bodenbelag aus schwarzen Schieferplatten. Beherrschendes Element des Wohnraumes ist der schwarze Eisenkamin, dessen Rundungen eine Korrespondenz zu den Säulen des Wohnhofes andeuten.

5. Entrance court seen from north-west. On the right is the central building, on the left one of the dwelling unit. Both buildings are so placed that the solarium behind the entrance as well as the living room (not visible in this picture) are protected against the prevailing north-east Mistral. On their north and west sides, all the buildings are enclosed but for high strip windows.

6. The white-plastered walls are in deliberate contrast with the reinforced concrete framework which has been left its natural colour. Above them the undulated roof shell rises freely to provide a lively accent.

7. The main entrance, reached via a flight of steps, is set into a rubble wall.

5. Blick aus Nordwesten in den Eingangshof. Rechts der Zentralbau und links eines der Apartmenthäuschen. Beide Gebäude sind so gestellt, daß sie den hinter dem Eingang liegenden Sonnenhof und den auf dem Bild nicht sichtbaren Wohnraum gegen den meist aus Nordosten einfallenden Mistral schützen. Nach Norden und nach Westen sind alle Gebäude bis auf schmale Oberlichtbänder geschlossen.

6. Die weiß verputzten Mauern lassen das naturfarben belassene konstruktive Betongerüst hervortreten.

7. Der Haupteingang, zu dem einige Stufen hinaufführen, ist in eine Bruchsteinmauer eingefügt.

8. The large solarium on the south side. Below the stairs in the background is the entrance to the lower floor of the dwelling units.

9. View from the west. The slope is broken by a long concrete wall which serves, at the same time, as an visual link between the different living areas.

10. The individual dwelling units too, are opened up with large, storey-high windows on the south side.

8. Blick in den großen Sonnenhof auf der Südseite. Unter der Treppe der Zugang zum Untergeschoß eines der Apartmenthäuschen.

9. Ansicht von Westen. Der Geländeabfall wird durch eine lange Mauer aufgefangen, die zugleich die verschiedenen Wohnflächen optisch aneinander bindet.

10. Auf der Südseite sind auch die Apartmenthäuser durch große, geschoßhohe Fenster nach außen geöffnet.

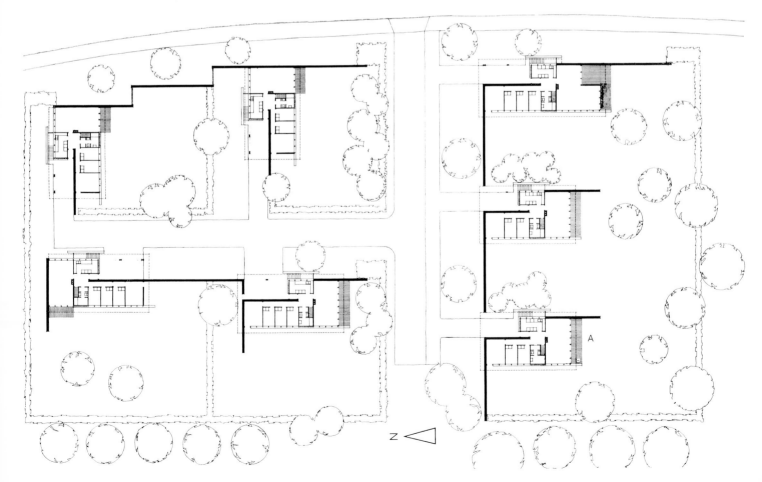

1. South side of one ot the houses (marked A in the site plan) with living room porch.
2. Site plan showing the road layout and the arrangement of the gardens.
3. Porch, seen from the west. On the east side, the storey-high brick wall provides privacy. On the west side, the boundary of the outdoor sitting area is marked by the extension of the window wall.

1. Blick von Süden auf eine Wohnraumterrasse (im Lageplan Haus A).
2. Lageplan mit Wegführung und Gartengestaltung.
3. Die Terrasse von Westen gesehen. Nach Osten gibt die geschoßhohe Mauer Schutz. Der Freisitzplatz wird auf der Westseite von der weitergeführten gemauerten Fensterbrüstung begrenzt.

Seven bungalows near Rungsted, Denmark
Architects: Jörgen Bo and Vilhelm Wohlert

This group of bungalows occupies a large, tree-studded site in a northern suburb of Copenhagen. Since, in this case, the sale of individual lots was precluded by the local building bye-laws, the architects tried to design the houses so that they are similar in appearance, without being monotonously identical. By varying the arrangement and number of rooms, even the plans themselves provide sufficient margin for individual features. Moreover, the overall arrangement is such that each of the houses has adequate private open space. Yet the seven bungalows fit into the landscape more satisfactorily than if each owner had suited his own taste. Access to the nearly level meadow is provided by a T-shaped service road, around which the houses are arranged in three groups. Storey-high brick walls, painted white, serve to connect and, at the same time, to separate the individual houses. They project into the open space, thus indicating the zones belonging to each house. They do this without, however, providing a physical separation which would merely over-emphasize the close proximity of the houses and would not accord with the Danish style of living where the neighbour's privacy is respected as a matter of course. All the living rooms and bedrooms face south and west. The plans are designed on similar principles. Differences merely arise from the size and number of the rooms. In each case, the living room occupies approximately one-third of the whole floor area. Another third is occupied by the bedrooms and bathroom, and the last third by kitchen and car port which is integrated with the house. A free-standing brick wall projected into the house screens the bedroom area from the carport and kitchen. Access is through the car port to the centrally placed hall from which all the rooms are accessible. The cellars can only be reached by outside stairs. The roof, overhanging on all sides, provides several covered outdoor sitting spaces. Construction: combination of load bearing brick walls and a post-and-beam system. Flat timber roof, untreated wooden ceilings and floors except in the hall where the flooring consists of red ceramic tiles. All joinery is dark stained.

Sieben Häuser bei Rungsted, Dänemark
Architekten: Jörgen Bo und Vilhelm Wohlert

Das große Baumgrundstück, auf dem die Gruppe von ebenerdigen Einfamilienhäusern errichtet wurde, liegt nördlich von Kopenhagen. Da die Bauvorschriften in diesem Fall den Verkauf in einzelnen Parzellen verboten, erstrebten und fanden die Architekten eine Lösung, bei der sich die verschiedenen Häuser zwar im Äußeren gleichen, ohne daß jedoch diese Gleichheit zu völliger Gleichmacherei führt. Durch die Variierung der Grundrisse und die wechselnde Anzahl der Zimmer ist schon vom Plan her der individuellen Entfaltung ausreichend Spielraum gegeben; zudem räumt die Gesamtdisposition jedem Haus genügend privaten Freiraum ein. Dabei fügen sich die sieben Baukörper besser in die Landschaft, als wenn jeder Bauherr seinem eigenen Geschmack gefolgt wäre. Die fast ebene Wiese wird durch eine T-förmige Stichstraße erschlossen, um die die Häuser in drei Gruppen angeordnet sind. Geschoßhohe, weiß getünchte Backsteinmauern verbinden und trennen die verschiedenen Bauten. Sie stoßen in den Grünbereich vor, den sie andeutungsweise in einzelne, jedem Haus zugeordnete Freiflächen gliedern. Eine vollständige Trennung ist jedoch nicht vorgesehen; sie würde die enge Nachbarschaft zu sehr betonen und ist auch nach dänischem Lebensstil nicht notwendig, da die Privatsphäre des Nachbarn hier ganz selbstverständlich respektiert wird. Alle Häuser sind mit ihren Wohn- und Schlafräumen nach Süden und Westen orientiert. Die Grundrißgestaltung folgt einem einheitlichen Prinzip. Unterschiede ergeben sich lediglich nach Größe und Zahl der Zimmer. Der Wohnraum nimmt jeweils etwa ein Drittel der Grundfläche ein. Von den beiden weiteren Dritteln entfällt eines auf die Schlafräume mit dem Bad und das zweite auf die Küche und den Wageneinstellplatz, der in den Baukörper integriert ist. Eine in das Haus hineingezogene Backsteinmauer schirmt den Schlafteil gegen Wagenplatz und Küche ab. Der Zugang erfolgt vom Wageneinstellplatz aus über die zentrale Diele, die die Räume erschließt. Die Keller sind jeweils nur über eine Außentreppe zugänglich. Das ringsum auskragende Dach schafft mehrere überdeckte Freisitzplätze. Konstruktion: Kombination von tragenden Backsteinmauern mit Stützensystem. Flachdach in Holzkonstruktion, Holzböden und Holzdecken natur belassen. In der Diele rote Keramikplatten als Fußboden.

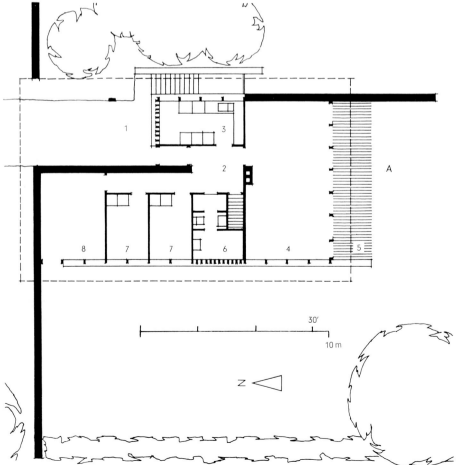

4. North side of the three bungalows occupying the southern part of the site. The roof canopies mark the house entrances. The carport faces the bedroom wing of the adjacent house.

5. Plan of House A. Key: 1 car port, 2 entrance and hall, 3 kitchen, 4 living room, 5 porch, 6 bathroom and W.C., 7 children's room, 8 master bedroom.

6, 7. Two different views of the living room in House A. Top: Chairs and settee on the west side; through the window the extension of the window wall is seen as a free-standing wall in the garden. On the right, behind the recess next to the chimney flue, the open fireplace with its box-shaped metal cowl. Bottom: East part of living-room, forming the dining area. The rear wall and its projection into the garden are of the same material: – white, lime-washed bricks. The full-height windows facing the outdoor sitting area are divided by dark-stained timber posts. Parquet flooring, boarded ceiling.

8. Interior of the kitchen. Above the cooker is a ventilation hood. The house entrance can be watched through additional windows overlooking the car port.

9. The centrally placed hall with the solid partition wall between the entrance (centre of picture) and the bedroom corridor. Unpretentious materials: untreated wood for walls and ceilings, white-washed bricks, red ceramic floor tiles.

10. Cellar stairs in front of the kitchen.

4. Die Nordseite der im Südteil des Geländes gelegenen drei Häuser. Unter den auskragenden Dächern Einfahrt und Zugang zum Haus. Vom Wageneinstellplatz blickt man auf die Schlafraumfront des nächsten Hauses.

5. Grundriß von Haus A. Legende: 1 Wageneinstellplatz, 2 Eingang und Diele, 3 Küche, 4 Wohnraum, 5 Terrasse, 6 Bad und WC, 7 Kinderzimmer, 8 Elternschlafraum.

6, 7. Zwei Ansichten des Wohnraumes von Haus A. Oben: Blick auf die Sitzgruppe im Westteil und die Fensterbrüstung, die im Freien als Mauer weiterläuft. Rechts hinter dem Rücksprung neben dem Schornstein der offene Kamin mit kastenförmiger Rauchschürze aus Blech. Unten: der Ostteil des Wohnraums mit dem Eßplatz. Rückwand und Trennmauer im Garten sind aus dem gleichen Material, weiß geschlämmten Backsteinen. Raumhohe Fensterwand zum Freisitzplatz, unterteilt durch dunkel gebeizte Holzstützen. Parkettfußboden, Langriemendecke.

8. Blick in die Küche. Über dem Herd ein Wrasenabzug. Durch zusätzliche Fenster zum Wageneinstellplatz läßt sich der Eingang übersehen.

9. Die zentrale Diele mit der massiven Trennmauer zwischen dem Eingang (Bildmitte) und dem Flur zum Schlafteil. Schlichte Materialien: naturfarbenes Holz für Wände und Decke, weiß geschlämmte Backsteine, rote Keramikplatten für den Fußboden.

10. Die Treppe zu den Kellerräumen vor der Küche.

1. West side with south patio (right). With its continuous strip of windows extending over the whole length, the house is wide open towards garden and woods.
2. East patio and east front, seen from north.
3. Plan. Key: 1 entrance and hall, 2 study, 3 living room, 4 dining room, 5 play room, 6 children's bedrooms, 7 master bedroom, 8 bathroom and W.C., 9 utility room, 10 kitchen, 11 entrance patio, 12 car port, 13 south patio.
4. Entrance patio with car port.
5. The windows are inserted directly into the structural framework. Two sliding doors lead from the living room and from the playroom to the garden. The panels below the windows are covered by vertical boarding.

1. Westansicht mit dem Südhof (rechts). Mit einem über die ganze Fassadenlänge geführten Fensterband öffnet sich das Haus auf Garten und Wald.
2. Blick von Norden auf Osthof und Ostfassade.
3. Grundriß. Legende: 1 Eingang und Diele, 2 Studio, 3 Wohnraum, 4 Eßzimmer, 5 Spielzimmer, 6 Kinderzimmer, 7 Elternschlafraum, 8 Bad und WC, 9 Hauswirtschaftsraum, 10 Küche, 11 Eingangshof, 12 Wageneinstellplatz, 13 Südhof.
4. Blick in den Eingangshof mit Wageneinstellplatz.
5. Die Fenster sind zwischen die Konstruktionsachsen gespannt. Zwei Schiebetüren verbinden den Garten mit Wohnraum und Kinderzimmer. In den Brüstungsfeldern eine vertikale Holzschalung.

Architect's house at Søllerød, near Copenhagen
Architects: Paul Amentorp and Peer Haubroe

As the site is bordered by woods on the north and west sides and the access road is at the south-east corner, the architect Haubroe placed his house as far to the east as possible, creating an entrance patio on the east side. The oblong plan is longitudinally divided into a wider west side and a narrower east side; the latter contains a study, utility rooms and master bedroom. Superimposed on this longitudinal division is a transverse division by which the rooms are functionally combined into three groups: The northern-most third of the house is occupied by the living room facing west, the study facing east, and the main entrance. In the central part of the house are the dining area with adjacent play room and the kitchen with a utility room. The last third is occupied by bedrooms and bathroom. With this division of the house into three distinct areas, the possibility of mutual interference is minimized. On the other hand, by using sliding doors, the plan is kept so open that a large coherent living room can be created, extending from the study to the play room. Construction: load-bearing walls of brick, combined with timber framework construction. The flat roof rests on laminated beams which are left exposed. Oak flooring. Central heating.

Architektenhaus in Søllerød bei Kopenhagen
Architekten: Paul Amentorp und Peer Haubroe

Wald an der Grundstücksgrenze im Norden und Westen und die an der Südostecke mündende Zufahrtsstraße waren für den Architekten Haubroe Grund, sein Haus möglichst weit nach Osten zu stellen und vor der Ostseite einen Eingangshof zu schaffen. Da von Süden das Nachbarhaus dicht heranrückt, wurde auch hier eine geschoßhohe Sichtschutzmauer notwendig. Der langgestreckte rechteckige Grundriß ist längsgeteilt in eine breitere West- und eine schmälere Osthälfte, in der Studio, Wirtschaftsräume und Elternschlafraum untergebracht sind. Diese Längsgliederung wird durchdrungen von einer Querteilung, die die Räume nach dem funktionalen Ablauf des Wohnens in drei Gruppen zusammenfaßt: im nördlichen Hausdrittel liegen der nach Westen orientierte Wohnraum, das nach Osten orientierte Studio und der Haupteingang. Im Mittelteil des Hauses folgen Eßplatz mit anschließendem Spielzimmer und Küche mit Hauswirtschaftsraum. Schlafräume und Bad nehmen das letzte Drittel ein. Die so gebildeten drei Zonen reduzieren die möglichen Störungen zwischen den Wohnbereichen auf ein Minimum. Andererseits ist der Grundriß durch die Verwendung von Schiebetüren so offen gehalten, daß sich ein großer zusammenhängender Wohnraum schaffen läßt, der vom Studio bis zum Spielzimmer reicht. Konstruktion: Tragende Wände aus Ziegelmauerwerk, kombiniert mit Holzständerfachwerk. Innenwände verputzt oder Holzpanels. Flachdach auf sichtbar belassenen Schichtholzbalken. Böden Eichenparkett. Zentralheizung.

N

6. Entrance patio with partly covered car port. On the east side of the house are the main entrance (background) and the secondary entrance to the utility room.

7. The south patio can be reached directly through a sliding door from the bedroom corridor. Privacy is ensured by a storey-high wall.

8. Living room. Next to the fireplace is the passage to the study, in the foreground to the right the door leading to the hall. In front of the roof beam just visible on top of the picture runs a sliding door by which the living room can be separated from the dining room. With the exception of the black painted roof beams, the timber work is kept in different shades of grey.

9. The hatch between kitchen and dining room also serves as breakfast table.

10. A view from the living room through dining room and play room towards the bedroom corridor. Built-in cupboard units and wood panels serve as partitions and sub-divide the doorless central zone of the house.

6. Eingangshof mit teilweise überdachtem Wageneinstellplatz. In der Ostfassade Haupt- und Nebeneingang (vorn) zum Hauswirtschaftsraum.

7. Den Südhof kann man über eine Schiebetür zum Flur vor den Schlafräumen direkt erreichen. Gegen Einblick schützt die geschoßhohe Mauer.

8. Blick in den Wohnraum. Neben dem Kamin der Durchgang zum Studio, rechts vorn die Tür zur Diele. Vor dem oben im Bild sichtbaren Deckenbalken läuft die Schiebetür, mit der sich der Wohnraum zum Eßzimmer hin schließen läßt. Das Holzwerk ist, mit Ausnahme der schwarz gestrichenen Deckenbalken, in verschiedenen Grautönen gehalten.

9. Die Durchreiche von der Küche zum Eßzimmer dient gleichzeitig als Frühstücksplatz.

10. Blick aus dem Wohnraum über Eßzimmer und Spielzimmer in den Flur vor den Schlafräumen. Einbauschränke und Wände aus Holzpaneelen trennen die Räume und dienen im mittleren, türenlosen Bereich des Hauses als Raumteiler.

1. Seen from north-east, the house is partly hidden in the slope. In the foreground is the nursery wing; to the right of it the walled courtyard from which the children's rooms receive their daylight. Behind the wall on the left is the swimming pool.
2. View of the articulated and open south side, with the guest-house-cum-garage on the left.
3. Facade detail. Eaves and verges are faced with copper sheeting. Between the heads of the roof beams are narrow toplight windows.

1. Von Nordosten gesehen verschwindet das Haus weitgehend im Abhang. Im Vordergrund der Kinderflügel; rechts anschließend der ummauerte Hof, über den die Kinderzimmer belichtet werden. Hinter der Mauer links das Schwimmbecken.
2. Ansicht der stark gegliederten und geöffneten Südseite. Links Gästehaus und Garage.
3. Detail der Fassade. Dachgesims und Stirnseiten der Dachbalken sind mit Kupferblech verkleidet. Zwischen den Balkenköpfen schmale Oberlichter.

House at Novaggio, Switzerland
Architects: Alberto Camenzind and Bruno Brocchi. Associate: Robert Sennhauser

Taking advantage of the slope of the site, situated at a bend of the road below Novaggio, the house is so embedded in the slope that the interiors cannot be seen from the road nor from neighbouring houses. From the west, north and east, nothing can be seen of the house but window-less, rubble walling. With the exception of the nursery wing which faces into a high-walled courtyard on the west side, all the rooms face south. The centre of the house is the living room, flanked by a summer sitting room in the form of a covered porch which is recessed into, and integrated with, the house. Behind the solid wall forming the east side of the porch is the master bedroom which has full-height corner windows and a direct exit to the swimming pool on its east side. The swimming pool, in its turn, is flanked by storey-high walls on its north and east sides. On the north side of the living room, along a corridor, are entrance hall and cloak room, a storage room, and the kitchen with larder and breakfast bar. The three children's room in the projecting north wing are separated from the remainder of the house by bathroom, boiler room and closet. On the west side is a completely self-contained, smaller building with a guest room and the garage, linked with the main building merely by joining the garage wall with that of the entrance hall. In this way, a second patio is created between the two parts of the house which must be crossed by the guests when they enter the main building. External and internal appearance of the house are dominated by the use of simple materials left in their natural state; rubble walling of local stone, roof members and posts of timber. Construction: Loadbearing walls combined with timber posts on the south side. The flat timber roof structure rests on glued laminated girders, left visible. Square clay tile flooring.

Haus in Novaggio, Schweiz
Architekten: Alberto Camenzind und Bruno Brocchi. Mitarbeiter: Robert Sennhauser

Das Gefälle des unterhalb von Novaggio an einer Straßenbiegung gelegenen Grundstückes wurde dazu benutzt, das Haus so in den Hang einzubetten, daß es weder von der Straße noch von den benachbarten Häusern her eingesehen werden kann. Von Westen, Norden und Osten aus gesehen zeigt das Gebäude nur fensterlose Bruchsteinmauern. Es öffnet sich ausschließlich nach Süden, mit Ausnahme der Räume des Kinderflügels, die nach Westen auf einen geschoßhoch ummauerten Hof orientiert sind. Das Zentrum der ganzen Anlage bilden der Wohnraum und der anschließende, in das Haus einbezogene Sommerwohnraum, eine hinter der Fassade liegende überdeckte Terrasse. Hinter der massiven Mauer, die ihren östlichen Abschluß bildet, folgt der Elternschlafraum, der über raumhohe Eckfenster belichtet wird und einen direkten Ausgang zum auf der Ostseite anschließenden Schwimmbecken hat. Das Schwimmbecken ist seinerseits wieder in einen geschoßhohen L-förmigen Mauerzug eingefügt. Auf der Nordseite der Wohnraumgruppe liegen längs eines Flurs Eingang mit Garderobe, Abstellraum und die Küche mit Speisekammer und Frühstücksbar. Drei Kinderzimmer im nach Norden vorstoßenden Querflügel sind gegen die übrigen Räume des Hauses durch Bad, Heizung und Schrankraum isoliert. Als völlig selbständiger Gebäudeteil liegt im Westen ein zweiter, kleinerer Hausblock, der ein Gästezimmer und die Garage aufnimmt. Er ist dadurch an das Haupthaus angebunden, daß die Nordwand der Garage in die Eingangsdiele hereingezogen wurde. Auf diese Weise entsteht zwischen den beiden Baukörpern ein weiterer Gartenhof, den die Gäste überqueren, wenn sie zum Hauptgebäude gehen. Die bauliche Erscheinung dieses Hauses wird im Äußeren wie im Inneren bestimmt durch die Verwendung einfacher, naturbelassener Materialien: Bruchsteine heimischer Gesteinsarten für Mauern, Holz für Flachdach und Stützen. Konstruktion: Tragende Mauern kombiniert mit Holzständern in der Südfassade. Dach Holzkonstruktion auf sichtbar belassenen lamellengeleimten Unterzügen. Böden mit quadratischen Spaltklinkerplatten belegt.

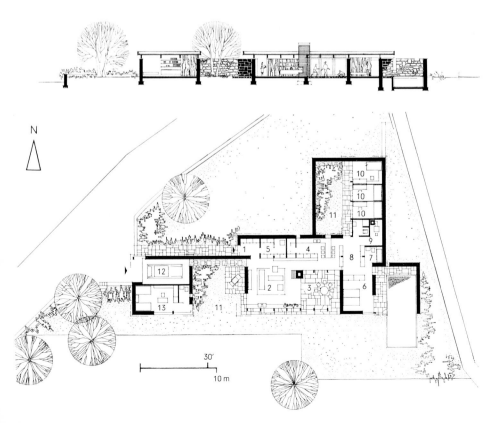

4. South side, seen from south-east, with the road and village in the background. On the far left is the guest house with its patio, then come by the four bays of the main building occupied by living room and porch. Behind the solid wall is the master bedroom with its corner window and door leading to the swimming pool.

5. Section and plan. Key: 1 entrance, 2 living room, 3 porch, 4 kitchen with dining area and larder, 5 storage room, 6 master bedroom, 7 bathroom and shower bath, 8 cupboard room, 9 boiler room, 10 children's room, 11 patio, 12 garage, 13 guest room.

4. Die Südseite von Südosten. Im Hintergrund Straße und Dorf. Links das Gästehaus mit Gartenhof, daran anschließend im Hauptgebäude die vier Fensterachsen des Wohnraums und des offenen Sommerwohnraums. Hinter der Wandscheibe der Elternschlafraum mit Eckfenster und Tür zum Schwimmbecken.

5. Schnitt und Grundriß. Legende: 1 Eingang, 2 Wohnraum, 3 Terrasse, 4 Küche mit Eßplatz und Speisekammer, 5 Abstellraum, 6 Elternschlafraum, 7 Bad und Dusche, 8 Schrankraum, 9 Heizraum, 10 Kinderzimmer, 11 Hof, 12 Garage, 13 Gastzimmer.

6. Living room with island fireplace which is placed exactly in the centre of the living area.
7. Porch, with the dining area in the background.
8. Corridor connecting the bedrooms with the entrance. Inside the living room, the passage is marked by the carpet edge. On the left is the porch. The sliding doors can be pushed aside so that the rooms can be combined.

9. One of the children's rooms with built-in furniture. Additional daylight is provided by the clerestory windows.

6. Der Wohnraum mit dem offenen Kamin, der genau im Zentrum des Wohnbereiches steht.
7. Blick in den Sommerwohnraum; im Hintergrund der Eßplatz.

8. Der Verbindungsflur zwischen Schlafteil und Eingang. Im Wohnraum ist die Passage durch die Teppichkante markiert. Links der Sommerwohnraum. Schiebetüren ermöglichen ein Ineinanderfließen der Räume.
9. Eines der Kinderzimmer mit Einbaumöbeln. Der Raum erhält zusätzliches Tageslicht durch Oberlichtstreifen.

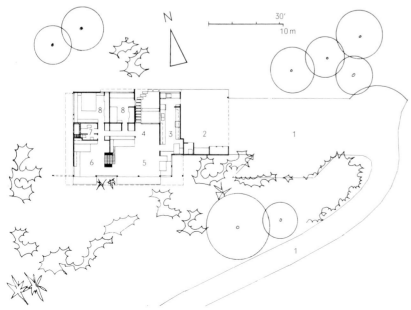

House for G. Serulnic near La Crescenta, California
Architect: Richard J. Neutra

The site, forming a shelf on a precipitous mountain slope, gave rise to considerable difficulties as it was first of all necessary to build an access road and to level the ground. But the efforts were more than compensated by the magnificent mountain panorama and the completely isolated position in an unspoilt landscape. A long and winding hillside road leads to the car port projecting on the east side of the house. From here, one may either enter through the adjacent kitchen, or use the main entrance courtyard on the north (mountain) side which is cut into the building as an open bay with a pool of water flanked by a path. The plan of the house is nearly square. Bedrooms, bathroom, entrance and kitchen are grouped in the northern half whilst the other half is taken up by the living quarters; these are sub-divided by fireplace and built-in furniture into a study and the living room proper which has dining bay. The south front, protected against sun and rain by the overhanging flat roof, consists entirely of full-height windows and sliding doors, conveying the impression of complete integration with the landscape even when the windows are closed. Construction: Wood posts and beams on concrete foundations. Gravel-strewn flat roof on timber beams. Ceilings and walls plastered white. Some birch faced wall panels.

Haus G. Serulnic bei La Crescenta, California
Architekt: Richard J. Neutra

Das Grundstück, ein stufenförmiger Einschnitt an einer steilen Bergflanke, bot erhebliche Schwierigkeiten, da erst einmal eine Zufahrt angelegt und das Terrain planiert werden mußte. Dieser Aufwand wird jedoch mehr als aufgewogen durch die weite Aussicht über das umgebende Gebirgspanorama und die völlig freie Lage in unberührter Natur. Über einen langen gewundenen Fahrweg erreicht man die Ostseite des Hauses mit dem vorgezogenen Wageneinstellplatz. Von hier aus betritt man entweder direkt die anschließende Küche oder benützt den auf der Nordseite, zum Berg hin liegenden offiziellen Eingang, der als offene Bucht mit Wasserbecken und Steg in den Baukörper eingeschnitten ist. Der Grundriß des Hauses ist annähernd quadratisch. Schlafräume, Bad, Eingang und Küche sind in der Nordhälfte zusammengefaßt, die andere Hälfte nimmt der Wohnraum ein, der durch den Kamin und Einbaumöbel in ein Studio und in den eigentlichen Wohnteil mit Eßecke unterteilt wird. Die Südfront, durch das auskragende Flachdach gegen Sonne und Regen geschützt, ist mit wandhohen Fenstern und Schiebetüren ganz in Glas aufgelöst. So entsteht auch bei geschlossenen Fenstern der Eindruck, unmittelbar in der Landschaft zu wohnen. Konstruktion: Holzskelett auf Betonfundament. Bekiestes Flachdach auf Holzbindern. Decken und Wände weiß verputzt. Einzelne Wandfelder mit Paneelen aus Birkenholz verkleidet.

1. South side of the house with the living room sliding doors open. Mounted in a pocket at the extreme edge of the roof are light fittings as well as an awning which extends over the whole length of the facade.
2. Plan. Key: 1 drive way, 2 car port, 3 kitchen, 4 entrance and hall, 5 living room, 6 study, 7 bathroom and W.C., 8 bedroom.
3. House entrance with car port; behind it the kitchen.

1. Blick auf die Südfront des Hauses mit den geöffneten Schiebetüren des Wohnraums. In der Vorderkante der Dachauskragung sind eine Leuchtwanne und ein Sonnensegel untergebracht, das über die ganze Fassadenlänge reicht.
2. Grundriß. Legende: 1 Zufahrt, 2 Wageneinstellplatz, 3 Küche, 4 Eingang und Diele, 5 Wohnraum, 6 Studio, 7 Bad und WC, 8 Schlafraum.
3. Die Zufahrt zum Haus mit dem Wageneinstellplatz, dahinter die querliegende Küche.

4. Living room, seen from the terrace. On the right is the kitchen hatch and, in front of it, an occasional table which can be raised to dining height. In the centre is the north entrance where the plants in the pool of water can be discerned through the frosted glass. Behind the large settee near the fireplace (left) is a birchwood panelled cupboard wall broken by a way through to the smaller bedroom.

5. In the entrance courtyard, the facade recesses to form a room-deep set-back with a pool of water and a narrow pathway leading to the main entrance door. On the left is the kitchen, on the right the outer door of the second bedroom which is also used as a guest room.

6. View from the dining area towards the fireplace which is open on three sides, and screens the study. Behind the settee on the right is the door to the main bedroom and bathroom.

4. Blick von der Terrasse in den Wohnraum. Rechts Durchreiche zur Küche. Davor der in der Höhe verstellbare Tisch der Eßecke. In der Mitte die Eingangstür der Nordseite, durch deren Mattglasscheiben die Pflanzen des Wasserbeckens erkennbar sind. Hinter der großen Couch am Kamin (links) eine birkenholzverkleidete Schrankwand mit dem Durchgang zum kleineren Schlafraum.

5. Im Bereich des Eingangs springt die Fassade um Zimmertiefe zurück und bildet eine Nische mit Wasserbecken und schmalem Steg zur Haustür. Links die Küche, rechts die Außentür des zweiten, auch als Besuchszimmer verwendbaren Schlafraums.

6. Blick vom Eßplatz auf den dreiseitig offenen Kamin, hinter dem das Studio liegt. Rechts hinter der Sitzbank die Tür zu Hauptschlafraum und Bad.

7. Southward view from the living room. When the glass sliding doors are open, exterior and interior merge freely.

8. The space of the living room is subdivided into study and lounge by the fireplace which has a cladding of selected natural stone.

9. The glass partition above the sunken bath reaches down to the bathtub rim; it will later be replaced by a glass sliding door, giving access to a solarium yet to be created. Here again, the plants outside can be discerned through the frosted glass.

10. Main bedroom with its large west window above the built-in book shelves.

7. Blick aus dem Wohnraum nach Süden. Bei geöffneten Glasschiebetüren fließen Außen- und Innenraum ungehindert ineinander.

8. Als Raumteiler zwischen Studio und Wohnraum dient der Kamin, der mit ausgesuchten Natursteinen verkleidet ist.

9. Das bis zum Rand der in den Boden eingelassenen Wanne reichende Badezimmerfenster soll später zur Glastür umgebaut werden und den Zugang zu einem noch zu schaffenden Sonnenhof ermöglichen. Auch hier schimmern die Pflanzen des Außenbereichs durch das Mattglas.

10. Der Hauptschlafraum mit dem großen Westfenster über dem eingebauten Bücherregal.

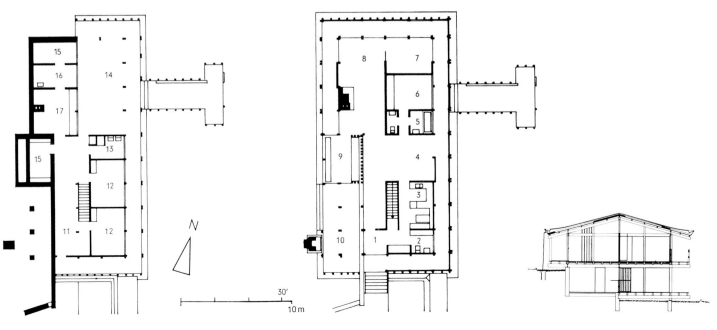

30'

10 m

House at Rude, Søholm, Denmark
Architect: Björn Börjeson

The two-storey hillside house stands on a peninsular site where the ground slopes down to the lake on the north and east sides. The main floor, glazed on all sides, is at upper ground level whilst the lower floor faces the lake towards east. The approach path leads from the western boundary of the site to the south side of the house which is entered via a few steps at main floor level. The hall, placed across the short side of the house, serves as the main circulation area. From the hall, a flight of stairs leads down to the lower floor; to the left of the stairs there is direct access to the dining and living rooms, to the right is the kitchen and, beyond it, the dining room which, at its north end, merges with the living room. On the west side, the living room is linked with the open terrace by a conservatory so that, throughout the house, the amenities can be adapted to suit season and weather. Facing the lake on the lower floor are two children's rooms and a shower bath, accessible from a large hall which also serves as hobby room. At the north-east corner of the lower floor, the house stands on stilts, thus providing a large covered terrace which is directly connected with the boat jetty. Utility rooms and cellars are concentrated in the west side of the lower floor. An outside flight of stairs at the end of the access path leads directly to the lower floor and lake shore. Construction: Timber posts with light-weight partitions. Slatetiled hipped roof with visible tarred roof beams. 'Thermopane' windows, panels below windows faced with white plastic sheet material. Lime-washed walls tinted a light sepia. Oak strip parquet flooring.

Haus in Rude, Søholm, Dänemark
Architekt: Björn Börjeson

Auf dem Grundstück, einer Halbinsel, die nach Norden und Osten zu einem See hin abfällt, wurde ein zweigeschossiges Hanghaus erbaut. Das Hauptgeschoß liegt, nach allen Seiten hin offen, auf dem oberen Geländeniveau, während das Untergeschoß nach Osten zum See hin orientiert ist. Der Zugang führt von der Westgrenze des Grundstücks zur Südseite des Hauses, das man über einige Stufen im Hauptgeschoß betritt. Die an der Stirnseite quergelegte Diele fungiert als Verteilerraum. Von hier aus führt links von der Treppe zum Untergeschoß ein direkter Zugang in den Wohnbereich. Auf der anderen Seite der Treppe liegt die Küche und dahinter das Eßzimmer, das mit dem Wohnbereich in der Nordwestecke eine große zusammenhängende Raumeinheit bildet. Auf der Westseite ist der Wohnraum durch den Wintergarten mit der offenen Terrasse verbunden, und so bieten sich in der Längsachse des Hauses je nach Jahreszeit und Wetter differenzierte Wohnmöglichkeiten. Auf der Seeseite des Untergeschosses liegen zwei Kinderzimmer und ein Duschraum. Sie werden über eine große Diele erschlossen, die gleichzeitig als Hobbyraum dient. An der Nordostecke des Untergeschosses steht das Haus auf Stützen, so daß sich hier eine große überdachte Terrasse ergibt, die direkt mit dem Bootssteg verbunden ist. Auf der Westseite des Untergeschosses sind Keller- und Wirtschaftsräume zusammengefaßt. Über eine Außentreppe am Ende des Zugangsweges ist das Untergeschoß und das Seeufer unmittelbar zu erreichen. Konstruktion: Holzstützen mit leichten Trennwänden. Schiefergedecktes Walmdach mit offenem Dachstuhl aus schwarz geteerten Balken. Thermopanefenster, Brüstungen mit weißen Kunststoffplatten verkleidet. Leicht nach Sepia getöntes geschlämmtes Mauerwerk. Parkettfußböden aus Eichenlangriemen.

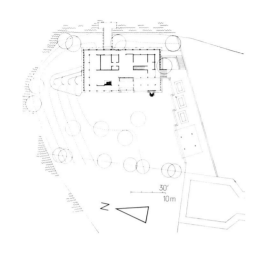

1. North-west side of the house. From this side, the house looks like an oblong bungalow. As many of the leaf-bearing and conifer trees as possible were preserved.
2. Plans of lower floor (left) and main floor and cross-section. Key: 1 entrance and hall, 2 W.C., 3 kitchen with breakfast corner, 4 dining room, 5 bathroom, 6 master bedroom, 7 study, 8 living room, 9 conservatory, 10 terrace, 11 hobby room, 12 children's room, 13 bathroom, 14 terrace, 15 cellar, 16 laundry, 17 boiler room.
3. Site plan. Along the front part of the access road, paved with ceramic slabs, stand the four columns which support the roof of the open-sided car port.

1. Ansicht von Nordwesten. Von dieser Seite aus wirkt das Haus wie ein langgestreckter eingeschossiger Baukörper. Der auf dem Gelände vorhandene Bestand an Laub- und Nadelbäumen wurde möglichst geschont.
2. Grundrisse von Untergeschoß (links) und Hauptgeschoß und Schnitt. Legende: 1 Eingang und Diele, 2 WC, 3 Küche mit Frühstücksplatz, 4 Eßzimmer, 5 Bad, 6 Elternschlafzimmer, 7 Arbeitszimmer, 8 Wohnraum, 9 Wintergarten, 10 Terrasse, 11 Hobbyraum, 12 Kinderzimmer, 13 Bad, 14 Terrasse, 15 Keller, 16 Waschküche, 17 Heizraum.
3. Lageplan. Im vorderen Teil des mit Keramikplatten gepflasterten Zugangsweges das auf vier Stützen stehende, an den Seiten offene Wagenschutzdach.

4

5

4. South-east side of the house. The apparent weightlessness of the structure is emphasized by the colour scheme: black, tarred beams, wall panels below windows faced with white plastic sheet material.

5. Lower floor terrace; in the background the boat jetty.

6, 7. Centre of the house, seen from the living room. On the left is the dining area, beyond the open sliding door is the kitchen, on the right the passage leading to the entrance hall. The light-weight partitions are covered with Japanese grass paper. The combined open area of the dining room and the living room conveys an impression of spaciousness.

6

7

8. The centre of the living room is the open fire-place, with brick walls and a natural stone base. In the background, the passage leading to the conservatory.

9. Terrace on the main floor with outdoor fire-place.

10. Conservatory and terrace at main floor level, with outdoor fireplace. The free-standing wall in the background, which ensures privacy from the road, forms an angle of 100° at the south-west corner where it links up with the house, forming the rear wall of the open terrace.

4. Die Südostseite des Hauses. Die Leichtigkeit der Konstruktion wird durch die Farbgebung – schwarz geteerte Balken, Brüstungen aus weißen Kunststoffplatten – betont.

5. Terrasse des Untergeschosses mit Bootssteg.

6, 7. Blick aus dem Wohnraum in die Mitte des Hauses. Links der Eßplatz, hinter der geöffneten Schiebetür die Küche, rechts der Verbindungsraum zur Eingangsdiele. Die leichten Trennwände sind mit japanischen Grastapeten beklebt. Der Wohnbereich bildet zusammen mit dem Eßplatz ein nach allen Seiten hin offenes, großzügig wirkendes Raumkontinuum.

8. Zentrum des Wohnbereichs ist der offene Kamin aus Ziegelmauerwerk mit Natursteinsockel. Im Hintergrund der Durchgang zum Wintergarten.

9. Terrasse des Hauptgeschosses mit Außenkamin.

10. Blick auf Wintergarten und Terrasse des Hauptgeschosses mit frei stehendem Außenkamin. Die Sichtschutzmauer gegen den Zugangsweg ist in der Südwestecke um 100° abgewinkelt und in das Haus hineingezogen, wo sie die Rückseite der offenen Terrasse bildet.

8

9

10

House at Pymble, New South Wales, Australia
Architect: Harry Seidler and Associates

The house, erected on a sloping three-acre site, is designed for a family with grown-up children. The slope has been utilised by adopting a split-level design. Extensions of the house walls and retaining walls give privacy to outdoor spaces and plastic interest to the otherwise simple shape of the building. The entrance is on the mountain side, next to the car port which forms part of the house. A screen of rubble walling leads to the entrance proper. The stonepaved entrance hall is open to the dining area on its left. The east side of the adjacent kitchen faces on to a utility patio. From the hall, stairs lead to the two-storey, valley-side of the house. On the lower floor are the living room with its covered outdoor terrace and on the east side the maid's room and shower room which can only be reached from outside. All the upper floor rooms face south. Between the master bedroom and the two rooms for the children, a study (also used as a guest room) with a balcony has been inserted. Construction: Load-bearing walls of buff-coloured facing bricks. Screen walls and fireplace of random rubble sandstone. Reinforced concrete panels; timber, joisted roof; internal walls boarded in ash; floor covering of plastic tiles and close carpeting.

Haus in Pymble, Neusüdwales, Australien
Architekt: Harry Seidler & Associates

Das auf einem abfallenden Grundstück von 1 ha Größe errichtete Haus für eine Familie mit erwachsenen Kindern wurde unter Ausnutzung der Hangneigung mit halbgeschossig gegeneinander versetzten Stockwerken erstellt. Dadurch, daß die über den Hausblock hinaus verlängerten Wände und Stützmauern geschützte Außenräume bilden, bekommt das sonst einfach gehaltene Gebäude eine reichere plastische Form. Der Zugang liegt auf der Bergseite, neben dem in das Haus einbezogenen Wageneinstellplatz. Eine Schirmwand aus Bruchsteinen führt zum Eingang hin. Die plattenbelegte Eingangsdiele ist nach links zum Eßplatz offen. Die anschließende Küche öffnet sich nach Osten auf einen Wirtschaftshof. Von der Diele aus wird der zweigeschossige, talseitige Teil des Hauses über eine Treppe erschlossen. Im Untergeschoß befinden sich der Wohnraum mit dem überdeckten Freisitzplatz und das nur von außen auf der Ostseite zugängliche Mädchenzimmer mit Duschraum. Alle Räume des Obergeschosses sind nach Süden orientiert. Zwischen den Elternschlafraum und die beiden Räume für die Kinder wurde noch ein Arbeits- und Besuchszimmer eingeschoben, das sich auf einen Balkon öffnet. Konstruktion: Tragende Wände in Sichtmauerwerk aus gelblichen Backsteinen. Schirmmauern und Kamin aus bruchrauhem Sandstein. Armierte Betondecken. Dach Holzkonstruktion. Innenwände mit Eschenholz verschalt. Boden Kunststoff-Fliesen und Spannteppiche.

1. South side, with the projecting balcony of the study.
2. The single-storey entrance side. The slope of the single-pitch roof (which is covered with white mineral-surfaced roofing) is to the slope of the hill.

1. Die Südseite mit dem auskragenden Balkon des Arbeitszimmers.
2. Die eingeschossige Eingangsseite. Die Neigung des Pultdaches (mit weißer Kiespappe beklebt) verläuft entgegengesetzt zur Hangneigung.

3. View from the dining area into the living room, with the covered terrace in the background.

3. Blick vom Eßplatz in den Wohnraum mit anschließender überdeckter Terrasse.

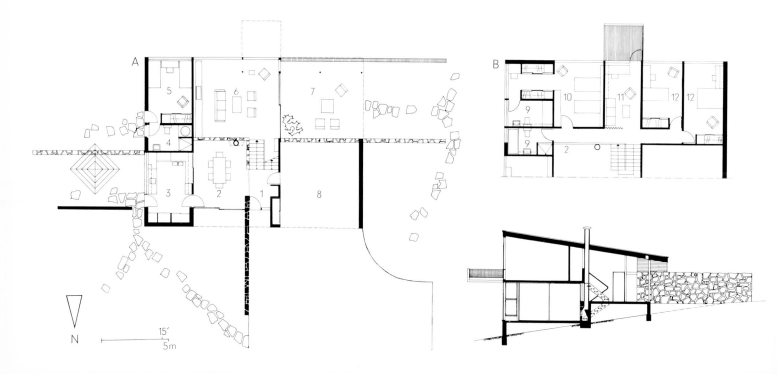

4. Section and plans of the entrance (lower) floor (A) and upper floor (B). Key: 1 entrance and hall, 2 dining area, 3 kitchen, 4 shower room, 5 maid's room, 6 living room, 7 terrace, 8 garage, 9 bathroom, 10 master bedroom, 11 study and guest room, 12 bedroom.
5. View from the upper floor gallery on to the dining area. In the background are the door and hatch from the kitchen. The rubble walling, the floor slabs of natural stone and the wall of the stairs leading to the lower floor define the entrance area.
6, 7. All the upper floor rooms are accessible from the gallery which is open to the dining area. Considerable spatial effect has been achieved by making the split-level arrangement visible. From the entrance, one is able to see not only the living room on the lower floor (across the dining area), but also, if the curtain is drawn back (Fig. 7), the study on the upper floor (across the gallery).
8. Garage and entrance wall, seen from the west.

4. Schnitt und Grundrisse von Eingangs- und Untergeschoß (A) und Obergeschoß (B). Legende: 1 Eingang und Diele, 2 Eßplatz, 3 Küche, 4 Dusche, 5 Mädchenzimmer, 6 Wohnraum, 7 Terrasse, 8 Garage, 9 Bad, 10 Elternschlafraum, 11 Arbeits- und Gastzimmer, 12 Schlafraum.
5. Blick von der Galerie des Obergeschosses auf den Eßplatz. Im Hintergrund die Tür zur Küche und die Durchreiche. Bruchsteinmauerscheibe und Bodenbelag aus Natursteinplatten umschreiben den Eingangsbereich.
6, 7. Alle Räume des Obergeschosses werden von der zum Eßplatz hin offenen Galerie erschlossen. Eine besondere räumliche Wirkung ergibt sich durch die sichtbar gemachte Geschoßversetzung. Man blickt vom Eingang über den Eßplatz sowohl in den Wohnraum des Untergeschosses, wie auch über die Galerie, bei geöffnetem Vorhang (Bild 7), in das Arbeitszimmer.
8. Blick von Westen auf Garage und die zum Eingang hinführende Bruchsteinmauer.

House for H. Grelling, near Ascona, Switzerland
Architect: Richard J. Neutra. Associates: Christian Trippel and Bruno Honegger

1, 2. East side of the house, forming the main frontage. The lower floor entrance is to the right of the stairs leading to the balcony. On the extreme right is the guest suite, above it the upper floor bedroom with its corner terrace.
3. View from the south. Above the garage is the living room balcony and, behind the solid wall, the dining room.

1, 2. Blick von Osten auf die Hauptfront. Im Untergeschoß, rechts von der Treppe zum Balkon, der Eingang. Ganz rechts das Gästeapartment, darüber der Schlafraum des Wohngeschosses, dessen Ecke als Balkon ausgespart ist.
3. Ansicht von Süden. Über der Garage der umlaufende Balkon vor dem Wohnraum. Hinter der Mauerscheibe das Eßzimmer.

The two-storey residence occupies a site above Lago Maggiore with a steep downwards slope from east to west. It is surrounded by wood land so that the panorama is confined to the lake. There are two approaches from the valley; one by the driveway which leads to the garage entrance in the south, and one by the winding footpath which affords fresh views of the house at every turn. It leads to the lower floor entrance of the main front between a pool and a stairway. Apart from utility rooms, the lower floor contains a suite for guests, consisting of two rooms, bathroom and kitchenette. The upper floor is reached either via the outer stairway leading to the surrounding gallery or via a second flight of stairs inside the house. The house is divided lengthwise into a wider strip on the valley side and a narrower strip three steps higher on the mountain side. On this side are the dining room, kitchen, utility room, maid's room, cupboard room and bathroom. On the east side, facing the lake are living room and bedrooms. With the exception of a solid wall on the south side of the dining room, the entire east and south sides are glass-fronted. The living room is subdivided by an island fireplace and a folding door into two areas, the larger one for sitting, the smaller serving as study. Large glass sliding doors provide access to the partly covered balcony. A terrace is also provided for the main bedroom which is reached from the living room or from the upper floor hall. Construction: Lower floor: Load bearing walls of concrete. Upper floor: Structural steel framework. Marble flooring, fir ceiling. Air conditioning.

Haus H. Grelling bei Ascona, Schweiz
Architekt: Richard J. Neutra. Mitarbeiter: Christian Trippel und Bruno Honegger

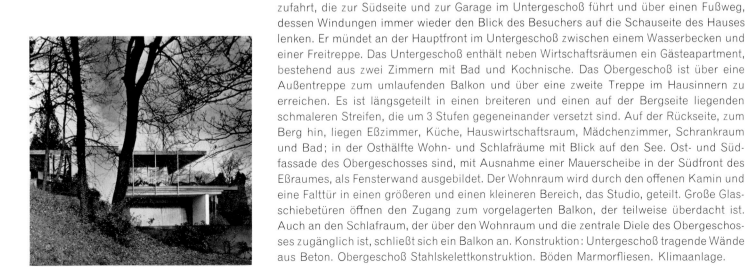

Das zweigeschossige Haus liegt auf einem steil von Osten nach Westen fallenden Grund-stück oberhalb des Lago Maggiore. Die parkartige Umgebung läßt nur den Blick auf den See frei. Man erreicht das Gebäude auf zwei Wegen, die im Tal beginnen: über die Auto-zufahrt, die zur Südseite und zur Garage im Untergeschoß führt und über einen Fußweg, dessen Windungen immer wieder den Blick des Besuchers auf die Schauseite des Hauses lenken. Er mündet an der Hauptfront im Untergeschoß zwischen einem Wasserbecken und einer Freitreppe. Das Untergeschoß enthält neben Wirtschaftsräumen ein Gästeapartment, bestehend aus zwei Zimmern mit Bad und Kochnische. Das Obergeschoß ist über eine Außentreppe zum umlaufenden Balkon und über eine zweite Treppe im Hausinnern zu erreichen. Es ist längsgeteilt in einen breiteren und einen auf der Bergseite liegenden schmaleren Streifen, die um 3 Stufen gegeneinander versetzt sind. Auf der Rückseite, zum Berg hin, liegen Eßzimmer, Küche, Hauswirtschaftsraum, Mädchenzimmer, Schrankraum und Bad; in der Osthälfte Wohn- und Schlafräume mit Blick auf den See. Ost- und Süd-fassade des Obergeschosses sind, mit Ausnahme einer Mauerscheibe in der Südfront des Eßraumes, als Fensterwand ausgebildet. Der Wohnraum wird durch den offenen Kamin und eine Falttür in einen größeren und einen kleineren Bereich, das Studio, geteilt. Große Glas-schiebetüren öffnen den Zugang zum vorgelagerten Balkon, der teilweise überdacht ist. Auch an den Schlafraum, der über den Wohnraum und die zentrale Diele des Obergeschos-ses zugänglich ist, schließt sich ein Balkon an. Konstruktion: Untergeschoß tragende Wände aus Beton. Obergeschoß Stahlskelettkonstruktion. Böden Marmorfliesen. Klimaanlage.

4, 5. Rear side of the house with the utility patio. Above the maid's room, the overhanging roof is replaced by a pergola. Continuous strip of sliding windows.

4, 5. Blick auf die Rückseite des Hauses mit dem Wirtschaftshof. Über dem Mädchenzimmer ist das auskragende Dach pergolaartig aufgelöst. Durchlaufendes Fensterband mit Schiebefenstern.

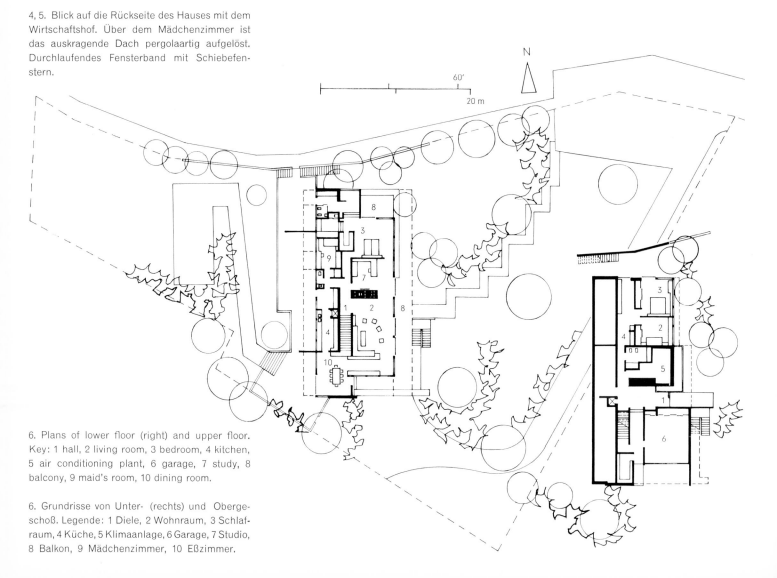

6. Plans of lower floor (right) and upper floor. Key: 1 hall, 2 living room, 3 bedroom, 4 kitchen, 5 air conditioning plant, 6 garage, 7 study, 8 balcony, 9 maid's room, 10 dining room.

6. Grundrisse von Unter- (rechts) und Obergeschoß. Legende: 1 Diele, 2 Wohnraum, 3 Schlafraum, 4 Küche, 5 Klimaanlage, 6 Garage, 7 Studio, 8 Balkon, 9 Mädchenzimmer, 10 Eßzimmer.

7. View from the living room balcony through the dining room towards the utility patio. With its flag paving, large windows, flower arrangements and slender roof supports, this part of the balcony has the appearance of an open pavilion.

8. Due to the elevation by three steps (see also Fig. 7), even the dining room enjoys a view on the lake across living room and balcony. Because of the large glass windows and sliding doors, interior and exterior seem to merge.

7. Blick vom Wohnbalkon durch das Eßzimmer in den Wirtschaftshof. Plattenbelag, große Glasflächen, Blumentrog und die schlanken Dachstützen machen diesen Teil des Balkons zu einem offenen Pavillon.

8. Durch die Höhenversetzung um drei Stufen (vergl. Bild 7) wird vom Eßplatz aus über Wohnraum und Balkon hinweg der Blick auf den See möglich. Die großen Glasfenster und -türen lassen Innen- und Außenraum ineinanderfließen.

9

10

9. From the dining room, three steps lead down to the living room level. The sitting area is separated and defined by a sideboard with built-in settee.

10 The straight stairway leads to the lower floor. The living room wall stops short of the ceiling offsetting the shaft-like character of the staircase. The dining area is segregated by means of a glass panel.

11. Chairs and table face the fireplace, which is covered with white marble tiles identical with the floor tiles. The fireplace, which can be closed by sliding doors, becomes a wall of the living room.

12. Folding doors give access to the study and to the adjacent bedroom. In this way, study and bedroom can be combined into a single suite.

13. Upper floor bedroom with storey-high corner windows. Behind the curtain is a sliding door leading to the north terrace where the overhanging roof beams form a pergola.

14. View from the bedroom to the dressing room three steps higher. Behind the white curtain is a sunken bath.

15. The living room of the guest suite on the lower floor has a large sliding door leading directly to the garden.

16. The long lower floor corridor gives access to the guest rooms. Next to the door, which leads to a small walled garden, is a narrow flower bed.

9. Vom Eßplatz führen drei Stufen auf die Ebene des Wohnraums herunter. Als Raumteiler und

11

12

13

14

Umgrenzung der Sitzgruppe dient ein Sideboard mit eingebauter Sitzbank.

10. Blick auf die gradläufige Treppe zum Untergeschoß. Die Wand zum Wohnraum ist nicht ganz bis zur Decke geführt. Damit wird die schachtartige Wirkung des schmalen Treppenhauses gemildert. Zum Eßplatz hin erfolgt der Abschluß durch eine Glasscheibe.

11. Die Sitzgruppe ist zum Kamin hin orientiert, der mit den gleichen weißen Marmorplatten belegt ist wie der Boden des Wohnraums. Der Ka-

min, der mittels Metallschiebetüren geschlossen werden kann, wird zur Wohnraumwand.

12. Falttüren öffnen den Zugang zum Studio und zu dem anschließenden Schlafraum. Studio und Wohnraum können so zu einem großen Raum zusammengefaßt werden.

13. Schlafraum im Wohngeschoß mit dem raumhoch verglasten Eckfenster. Hinter dem Vorhang Schiebetür zum vorgelagerten Nordbalkon, über dem der Rahmen der Dachkonstruktion pergolaartig auskragt.

14. Blick vom Schlafraum auf die drei Stufen höher liegenden Toilettenräume. Hinter dem weißen Vorhang die in den Fußboden eingelassene Badewanne.

15. Der Wohnraum des Gästeapartments im Untergeschoß steht über eine große Schiebetür direkt mit dem Garten in Verbindung.

16. Der längsgerichtete Flur im Untergeschoß dient als Zugang zu den Gästezimmern. Neben der Tür, die auf einen kleinen Gartenhof führt, ein schmales Pflanzenbecken.

15

16

1. South-west side. In the annex, under the lean-to roof on the left, is the guest room; adjacent to it is the storey-high wall surrounding the garden. Under the gable roof are the windows of the living room and of the main bedroom.
2. North side view, showing the house in its village setting to which its general design is adapted.
3. On the north-east side the house is, except for the main entrance, completely closed.

1. Ansicht von Südwesten. Im Anbau, links unter dem Pultdach, das Gästezimmer, daran anschließend die geschoßhohe Mauer des Gartenhofes. Unter dem Satteldach Wohnraum- und kleines Schlafraumfenster.
2. Die Gesamtansicht von Norden zeigt das Haus im Zusammenhang mit der Nachbarbebauung, an die es in den Grundformen angeglichen ist.
3. Die Nordostseite des Hauses ist bis auf den Haupteingang völlig geschlossen.

House for M. G. White at Askett, Buckinghamshire, England
Architect: Peter J. Aldington

For this site in the middle of a village, surrounded by anonymous 'Old English Cottage' architecture, the architect was required to design a house which would adapt itself externally as nearly as possible to the traditional rural building style of the near-by cottages, with their small windows, low ceilings and sloping roofs, yet would at the same time meet all the requirements of high modern living standards. The owners, a married couple, required two bedrooms, a dual-purpose room which could be used as a study or for guests, a living room large enough for parties, and a separate dining room. Without adopting a facile eclecticism, the architect created a house with a consistent and unaffected rustic quality not only in its outward appearance but also in its interior design. The living room, reached from the hall by a few steps, serves as central circulation space, horizontally as well as vertically. A flight of stairs connects with the two bedrooms on the upper floor. The guest room/study is on the ground floor to the right of the front entrance. Living room and sitting room which are on the same level, are flanked by the dining room and kitchen which are at a slightly lower level and separated from each other by built-in furniture. As the two-storey living room receives a good deal of light through the large window on the south-west side, it was possible, by adopting a fairly open plan, to rely on smaller windows for the other ground floor rooms without making these too dark. The large living room window became possible because the annex containing the entrance and guest room is confined to the lower (front) part of the house and is flanked in the rear by a walled garden, accessible from the living room. A similar, if smaller, reduction in width occurs on the east side where the lower part contains a separate kitchen entrance. Construction: Bearing walls are of brick, painted white. Lintels, ridges and verges are precast concrete blocks made with black Portland cement. Timber roof covered with concrete ribbed tiles. Visible structural timber of Douglas fir, walls and ceiling panelling, redwood. Electric floor heating.

Haus M. G. White in Askett, Buckinghamshire, England
Architekt: Peter J. Aldington

Auf einem Grundstück mitten im Dorf, umgeben von anonymer »Old English Cottage«-Architektur, war ein Haus zu erstellen, das sich im Äußeren weitgehend der ländlich-handwerklichen Bauweise der benachbarten Gebäude mit ihren kleinen Fenstern, niedrigen Räumen und spitzen Dächern anpassen und trotzdem alle Ansprüche eines gehobenen modernen Wohnstandards erfüllen sollte. Die Besitzer, ein Ehepaar, wünschten zwei Schlafräume, einen Mehrzweckraum, verwendbar als Studio und als Gastzimmer, einen Wohnraum, in dem auch größere Gesellschaften gegeben werden können, und ein separates Eßzimmer. Für dieses Raumprogramm schuf der Architekt, ohne in einen platten Eklektizismus zu verfallen, ein Gehäuse, das nicht nur außen, sondern auch in der Innenraumgestaltung eine einheitliche, ungekünstelte rustikale Note zeigt. Der Wohnraum, der von der Diele aus über einige Stufen zu erreichen ist, dient als zentrale Erschließungsfläche, sowohl horizontal wie auch vertikal. Eine Treppe schafft die Verbindung zu den beiden Schlafräumen im Obergeschoß. Der dritte Schlafraum, der als Gast- und Mehrzweckzimmer dient, liegt ebenerdig rechts vom Eingang. An den Wohnraum und das auf gleicher Höhe liegende Kaminzimmer schließen sich, wieder tiefer liegend, Eßzimmer und Küche an, wobei Küche und Eßplatz durch Einbaumöbel getrennt sind. Da der zweigeschossige Wohnraum durch sein großes Fenster auf der Südostseite relativ viel Licht erhält, können die übrigen Zimmer im Erdgeschoß bei entsprechend offenem Grundriß die gewünschten kleineren Fenster erhalten, ohne daß sie deshalb zu dunkel würden. Dieses große Fenster wurde möglich, weil der Anbau mit Eingang und Gastzimmer nur bis zur halben Firsthöhe geführt ist und dahinter ein ummauerter Gartenhof liegt, den man vom Wohnraum aus erreicht. Einen ähnlichen, aber kleineren Rücksprung zeigt auch die östliche Giebelseite; sie nimmt im Erdgeschoß einen separaten Zugang zur Küche auf. Konstruktion: Tragende Wände aus Ziegelmauerwerk, mit weißer Dispersionsfarbe gestrichen. Fensterstürze, Trauf- und Ortganggesimse als Betonfertigteile aus schwarzem Portlandzement ausgeführt. Dach Holzkonstruktion, gedeckt mit Beton-Falzziegeln. Sichtbare Holzteile im Innenausbau Douglaskiefer, Holzverschalungen von Wänden und Decken Redwood. Elektrische Fußbodenheizung.

4

5

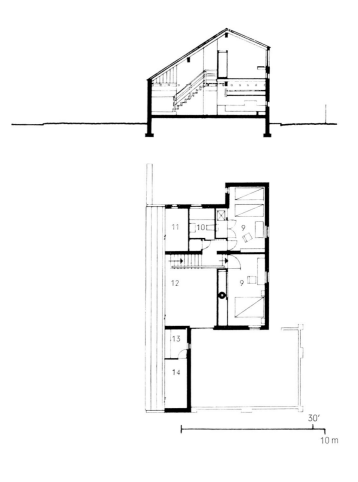

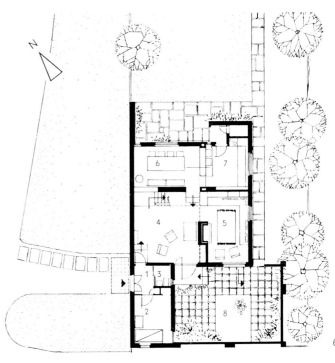

6

4. The narrow window above the kitchen entrance is that of the second bedroom on the upper floor. The black concrete lintels and verges provide visual accents.

5. South-west side, seen from the walled garden.

6. Section and plans of upper floor (centre) and ground floor. Key: 1 entrance, 2 study/guest room, 3 W.C., 4 living room, 5 sitting room, 6 dining room, 7 kitchen, 8 walled garden, 9 bedroom, 10 bathroom, 11 storage room, 12 upper space of living room, 13 upper space of hall, 14 storage room.

7, 8. From the entrance hall (Fig. 8), which extends right up to the sloping roof, a heavy door of solid timber boards gives access to the living room which is two steps higher (Fig. 7). In the background is the flight of stairs leading to the upper floor. Through the narrow horizontal glazed panel near the bottom landing of the stairs, the dining room is just visible; its ceiling joist provides a decorative motif in the wall. Above it in the wood-clad wall is the door leading to the storage room in the attic.

9. Living room and sitting room (right) are on the same level. On the left of the picture is the kitchen entrance. The exposure of the timber structure of the upper floor gallery is typical of the architect's intention 'to hide nothing of the structure but to create the character of the building by rigidly controlling the forms and dispositions of the structural elements, as did instinctively the craftsmen of old'.

4. Der Fensterschlitz über dem Kücheneingang belichtet den zweiten Schlafraum im Obergeschoß. Schwarze Betonfensterstürze und Giebelkanten setzen optische Akzente.

5. Blick vom Gartenhof auf die Südwestfassade.

6. Schnitt und Grundrisse von Obergeschoß (Mitte) und Erdgeschoß. Legende: 1 Eingang, 2 Gastzimmer, 3 WC, 4 Wohnraum, 5 Kaminzimmer, 6 Eßzimmer, 7 Küche, 8 Gartenhof, 9 Schlafraum, 10 Bad, 11 Abstellraum, 12 Luftraum Wohnraum, 13 Luftraum Eingangshalle, 14 Abstellraum.

7, 8. Vom Vorraum am Eingang (Bild 8), der bis unter die Dachschräge reicht, führt eine schwere Tür aus massiven Holzbrettern in den um zwei Stufen angehobenen Wohnraum (Bild 7). Im Hintergrund die Treppe zum Obergeschoß. Durch den schmalen horizontalen Fensterschlitz am Antritt der Treppe sieht man in das Eßzimmer, dessen Deckenbalken als ornamentales Motiv in der Treppenwand erscheinen. Darüber in der Holzverschalung die Tür zum Abstellraum unter der Dachfläche des Obergeschosses.

9. Wohnraum und Kaminzimmer (rechts) liegen auf gleicher Höhe. Links im Bild der Abgang zur Küche. Das Gebälk der Galerie im Obergeschoß ist bezeichnend für die Absicht des Architekten, »in allen Einzelheiten nichts von der Konstruktion zu verbergen, sondern – was die Handwerker früherer Zeiten instinktiv taten – den Charakter des Hauses durch eine Straffung der Formen und eine exakte Gliederung der Konstruktionselemente zu beeinflussen«.

10. Sitting room with built-in bench. The space below the upholstering can be used as a chest.

11. Kitchen and sitting room, seen from the dining room.

12. The kitchen has built-in fittings. Here, too, whitepainted brick walls alternate with wood panelled ones.

13. The shape of the long narrow dining room is emphasized by the long table and the benches.

10. Das Kaminzimmer mit der eingebauten Sitzbank. Der Raum unter den Polstern kann als Truhe verwendet werden.

11. Blick vom Eßzimmer auf Küche und Kaminzimmer.

12. Auch bei der Küche, deren Einrichtung eingebaut ist, wechseln weiß gestrichene Backsteinflächen mit Holz.

13. Das verhältnismäßig schmale Eßzimmer wird durch den großen Tisch und die Sitzbänke noch in seiner Längsrichtung betont.

14. A view of the second bedroom, placed in the north-east corner of the upper floor.
15–17. The main bedroom is two steps higher than the adjacent bedroom (cf. Fig. 16), matching the similar change in level on the ground floor. A cupboard unit with sliding doors, not extended to the ridge beams, separates the bedroom from the upper space of the living room. A solid table top with suspended drawers at the window serves as a dressing table.

14. Blick in den zweiten, in der Nordostecke des Obergeschosses liegenden Schlafraum.
15–17. Der Hauptschlafraum ist gegenüber dem benachbarten Schlafraum um zwei Stufen angehoben (siehe Bild 16), was der Niveauversetzung im Erdgeschoß entspricht. Ein nicht bis zum Firstbalken geführter Wandschrank mit Schiebetüren ist als Raumteiler zum zweigeschossigen Wohnraum verwendet. Vor dem Fenster wurde eine massive Holzplatte mit untergehängten Schubkästen als Toilettentisch angebracht.

1. View from west. The gentle slope of the single-pitch roof is set against the slope of the ground. Note the barbecue close to the chimney (bottom, right).
2. General view of the house from the river.
3, 4. Views from south-west and south-east. The main floor is set as a block on the smaller ground floor. Below it is a large sheltered terrace, adjoined by a swimming pool. The sculpture in the foreground of Fig. 4 is by Geoffrey Clarke.

1. Westansicht. Die schwache Schräge des Pultdaches verläuft entgegengesetzt zur Hangneigung. Rechts unten am Schornstein die Öffnung des Barbecue.
2. Südansicht des Hauses vom Fluß.
3, 4. Blick von Südwesten und Südosten. Das Wohngeschoß ist als Block auf das Erdgeschoß gesetzt. Darunter eine große, geschützte Terrasse mit anschließendem Schwimmbecken. Auf Bild 4 im Vordergrund eine Plastik von G. Clarke.

Architect's house at Beaulieu, England
Architect: Sir Basil Spence

The large site is on the bank of a river in the south of England. The ground slopes down from north to south and is studded with trees which were only cut down in the immediate vicinity of the house. The two-storey house, designed for the architect's own holiday use, is erected on a natural shelf of ground in the southern part of the site. On the west side of the ground floor are the garage, which also acts as a boat house, and a multi-purpose room, serving as workshop and utility room. The two solid walls placed at right angles to the slope, carry the upper floor, and are extended beyond the house. On the east side, they enclose a small outdoor sitting area. On the west side they enclose the entrance patio from which an outdoor stairway leads to the main floor. This upper floor projects far beyond the ground floor, and, if the loggia is included, covers an area more than twice that of the ground floor. It contains, in the northern half, the two bedrooms and the kitchen. The other half is taken up by the living room which is, on the south side, extended by a loggia running along the whole front of the house. Construction: Ground floor: white painted brickwork on concrete foundations. Upper floor: timber framed structure resting on two laminated soft wood cross beams. External and internal wall facing of wood. Afzelia hardwood strip flooring in all the rooms, except for quarry tiles in the service rooms. Timber roof.

Architektenhaus in Beaulieu, England
Architekt: Sir Basil Spence

Das große Grundstück liegt am Ufer eines Flusses in Südengland. Es fällt von Norden nach Süden und ist dicht mit Bäumen bewachsen, die nur im engeren Hausbereich gefällt wurden. Das als Ferienwohnsitz entworfene, zweigeschossige Gebäude ist auf einer natürlichen Geländestufe im südlichen Teil des Grundstücks errichtet. Das Erdgeschoß enthält im Westteil die Garage, in der auch die Boote aufbewahrt werden, und einen Mehrzweckraum, der als Werkstatt und als Hausarbeitsraum dient. Die beiden quer zur Hangneigung gestellten Mauerscheiben, auf denen das Obergeschoß ruht, sind über den Hausblock hinaus verlängert. Sie umschließen auf der Ostseite einen kleineren Freisitzplatz und auf der Westseite den Eingangshof, von dem aus man über eine Außentreppe in das Wohngeschoß gelangt. Es kragt weit über das Erdgeschoß aus und hat, rechnet man die Loggia dazu, mehr als die doppelte Grundfläche. In der Nordhälfte des Wohngeschosses sind die Schlafräume und die Küche untergebracht. Die zweite Hälfte wird vom Wohnraum eingenommen, dem eine über die ganze Hausfront reichende Loggia vorgelagert ist. Konstruktion: Erdgeschoß weiß gestrichene Ziegelmauern auf Betonfundament. Obergeschoß Holzrahmenkonstruktion auf zwei querliegenden Schichtholzbalken. Schalung innen und außen Holz. Böden in den Wohnräumen Afzeliariemen, in den Wirtschaftsräumen Steinplatten. Dach Holzkonstruktion.

5. Entrance patio. Under the stairs are oil tank and refuse bins. The brick wall on the right rises in steps towards the chimney and three cuts of different depth and width permit southward views towards the river. The wall on the opposite (left) side forms an angle towards north so as to enlarge the patio. Below the glass porch on the landing at the top of the stairs is a passage to the south terrace.

5. Blick in den Eingangshof. Unter der Treppe sind Öltank und Müllsammelraum untergebracht. Die Ziegelmauer rechts im Bild ist in der Höhe zum Schornstein hin gestuft. Drei Einschnitte verschiedener Tiefe und Breite gestatten den Blick nach Süden zum Fluß. Die gegenüberliegende Mauer, links im Bild, ist nach Norden abgeknickt, um den Hofbereich zu erweitern. Unter dem oberen Treppenpodest mit dem gläsernen Windfang ein Durchgang zur Südterrasse und zum Schwimmbecken.

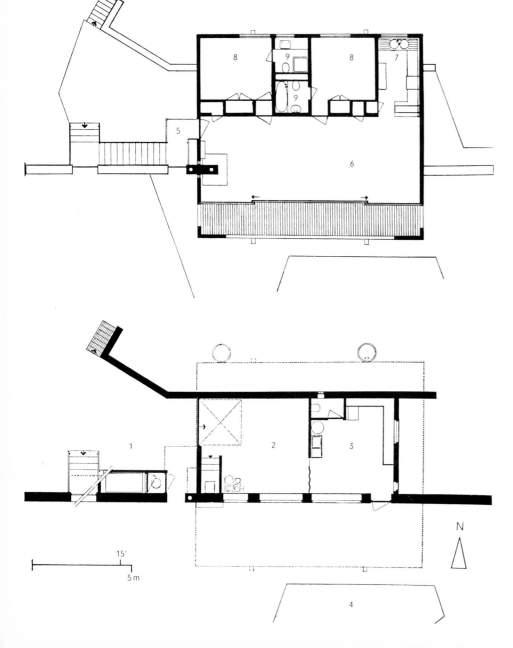

6. Plans of ground floor (bottom) and upper floor. Key: 1 entrance patio, 2 garage, 3 multi-purpose room, 4 swimming pool, 5 porch, 6 living room, 7 kitchen, 8 bedroom, 9 bathroom and W.C.
7. Motif on the floor of the swimming pool, designed by John Spence.

6. Grundrisse von Erdgeschoß (unten) und Wohngeschoß. Legende: 1 Eingangshof, 2 Garage, 3 Mehrzweckraum, 4 Schwimmbecken, 5 Windfang, 6 Wohnraum, 7 Küche, 8 Schlafraum, 9 Bad und WC.
7. Relief auf dem Boden des Schwimmbeckens, Entwurf John Spence.

8. Loggia and living room are connected by large wood-framed glass sliding doors so that the loggia can become part of the living room during the summer.

9. The element dominating the living room is the fireplace of white hammered concrete.

10. View from the dining area towards the fireplace. Below the narrow strip of toplighting is the entrance door. On either side of the flue are two storey-high strip windows.

8. Große Glasschiebetüren in Holzrahmen verbinden Loggia und Wohnraum, die so im Sommer zu einem Raum werden.

9. Das beherrschende Element des Wohnraums ist der Kamin. Feuerboden und Rauchschürze bestehen aus gehämmertem Beton.

10. Blick vom Eßplatz auf die Sitzgruppe vor dem Kamin. Unter dem schmalen Oberlicht die Eingangstür. Links und rechts vom Schornstein zwei geschoßhohe Glasstreifen.

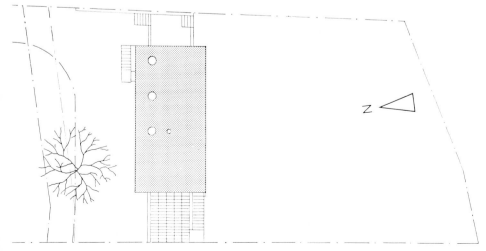

House for E. Siesby, Prinsessestien, Lyngby, Denmark
Architect: Arne Jacobsen

The house is erected on a site which slopes down about 50 ft. from north to south. In order to compensate for the differences in level and to obtain the best possible view across Lake Lyngby in the south, the main floor was placed on two solid walls across the slope. The long and narrow lower floor thus created can only be reached from outside, via a flight of stairs at the eastern end. As well as storage rooms and boiler room, it contains the owner's study which faces a small walled courtyard on the east side. Apart from the main entrance, reached via an external flight of stairs, the north side of the main floor, which is cantilevered at both longitudinal sides, has no doors or windows. All the rooms are grouped around the spacious hall which is used as a day nursery and has toplight domes. The three bedrooms and the kitchen face south whilst the living room, which extends over the entire width of the house, faces exclusively westwards, opening on to the garden terrace. Construction: On the lower floor brick walls rest wooden cross-beams at 2.2 metres (7'3") centres. The upper floor is a post-and-beam structure covered with boarding.

Haus E. Siesby, Prinsessestien, Lyngby, Dänemark
Architekt: Arne Jacobsen

Das Grundstück, auf dessen oberem Teil das Haus steht, fällt um etwa 15 m von Norden nach Süden. Um den Höhenunterschied auszugleichen und einen möglichst weiten Blick über den Lyngbysee im Süden zu ermöglichen, wurde das Wohngeschoß auf zwei quer zum Hang verlaufenden, völlig geschlossenen Mauerscheiben vom Boden abgehoben Das langgestreckte, schmale Untergeschoß, das auf diese Weise entsteht, ist nur von außen, über eine Treppe an der Ostecke, zugänglich. Es enthält neben Abstellräumen und Heizung das Studio des Hausherrn, das von Osten über einen kleinen, ummauerten Hof belichtet wird. Bis auf den Hauseingang, den man über eine Außenentree erreicht, ist die Nordseite des an beiden Längsfronten auskragenden Wohngeschosses völlig geschlossen. Alle Räume sind um die geräumige Diele gruppiert, die tagsüber als Kinderspielzimmer dient und durch Oberlichtkuppeln belichtet wird. Die drei Schlafräume und die Küche sind nach Süden orientiert, während sich der über die ganze Hausbreite reichende Wohnraum ausschließlich nach Westen auf die Gartenterrasse öffnet. Konstruktion: Untergeschoß Ziegelmauerwerk, darüber querliegende Holzbalken in 2,2 m Abstand. Wohngeschoß holzverschalte Ständerkonstruktion.

1. South side of the house with the bedroom and kitchen windows. Behind the timber-clad part of the wall is the living room.
2. Site plan. The design was governed by the small width of the site (just under 70 ft.) and by local bye-laws prescribing safety distances for timber houses. Moreover, it was necessary not to interfere with the view from a house situated on a higher level.
3. The basement rooms behind the solid wall of the lower floor receive daylight through clerestory strip windows inserted between the 30 × 15 cm (approx. 12" × 6") beams whose cantilever sections are tapered.
4. Plans of main floor (top) and lower floor. Key: Main floor: 1 entrance, 2 hall and day nursery, 3 living room, 4 terrace, 5 kitchen, 6 bedrooms, 7 bathroom and W.C.; lower floor: 1 courtyard, 2 study.

1. Die Südseite des Hauses mit den Fenstern der Schlafräume und der Küche. Hinter der holzverschalten Wandscheibe liegt der Wohnraum.
2. Lageplan. Dem Entwurf waren Grenzen gesetzt durch die Grundstücksbreite (21 m) und durch die Vorschriften über den Sicherheitsabstand bei Holzhäusern. Außerdem durfte einem höhergelegenen Haus nicht die Aussicht genommen werden.
3. Die Kellerräume hinter der massiven Mauer des Untergeschosses erhalten Licht durch schmale Fensterschlitze zwischen den 30 × 15 cm starken, im auskragenden Teil abgeschrägten Balken.
4. Grundrisse von Wohngeschoß (oben) und Untergeschoß. Legende Wohngeschoß: 1 Eingang, 2 Diele und Spielflur, 3 Wohnraum, 4 Terrasse, 5 Küche, 6 Schlafräume, 7 Bad und WC. Untergeschoß: 1 Hof, 2 Bibliothek.

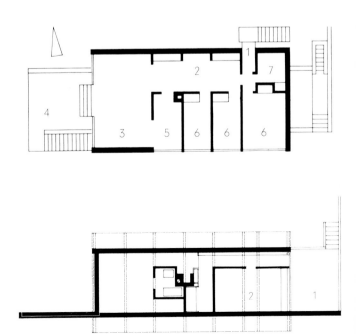

5. West terrace outside the living room. The difference in level between terrace and living room is due to the timber beams which support the upper floor. The top lights of the windows are the same size as the bottom panels. The eaves of the roof are accentuated by a narrow metal strip.
6. The north side is completely enclosed except for the main floor entrance, reached over a few steps.

5. Die Westterrasse vor dem Wohnraum. Der Niveauunterschied zwischen Terrasse und Wohnraum ergibt sich durch die Holzbalkenlage, auf der das Wohngeschoß ruht. Die Oberlichter sind in der Größe auf die Brüstungsfelder abgestimmt. Ein schmales Metallsims schließt den Hauskubus nach oben ab.
6. Die Nordseite ist völlig geschlossen. Den Eingang zum Wohngeschoß erreicht man über eine kurze, freitragende Treppe.

7. The living room placed across the house, seen from the terrace. The central window bay forms a sliding door. In the background of the living room are the day nursery on the left and the hatch from the kitchen on the right.

8. Playroom hall, with built-in cupboards, seen from the living room. Floor and ceiling are covered with wood battens of equal width.

9. The flap closing the kitchen hatch can be tilted down to serve as a breakfast table.

7. Blick von der Terrasse in den querliegenden Wohnraum. Die mittlere Fensterachse ist als Schiebetür ausgebildet. Im Hintergrund des Wohnraums links der Spielflur, rechts die Durchreiche zur Küche.

8. Blick aus dem Wohnraum in den Spielflur mit den eingebauten Schränken. Boden und Decke sind mit Holzriemen gleicher Breite verschalt.

9. Die Klappe, die die Durchreiche zur Küche schließt, dient geöffnet als Frühstückstisch.

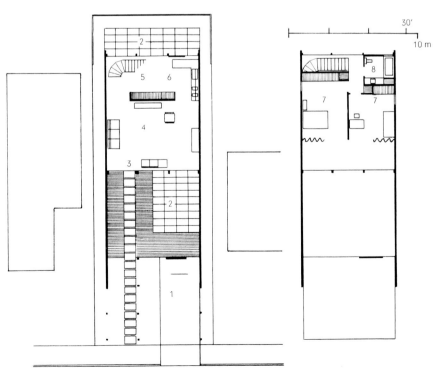

30'
10 m

1. View from the street. A two-storey high red-wood screen stands between house and car port.
2. Plans of ground floor (left) and upper floor. Key: 1 car port, 2 patio, 3 entrance, 4 living room, 5 dining area, 6 kitchen, 7 bedroom, 8 bathroom.

1. Ansicht von der Straße. Eine zweigeschossige Blende aus Rotholzplanken schirmt das Haus gegen den Wageneinstellplatz ab.
2. Grundrisse von Erdgeschoß (links) und Obergeschoß. Legende: 1 Wageneinstellplatz, 2 Terrasse, 3 Eingang, 4 Wohnraum, 5 Eßplatz, 6 Küche, 7 Schlafraum, 8 Bad.

House for R. Opdahl at Long Beach, California
Architects: Edward A. Killingsworth, Jules Brady and Associate

The plot, bordered by an older two-storey house on one side and a hardly more attractive one-and-a-half storey house on the other side, is no more than 30 ft. wide and 80 ft. long. In order to ensure maximum privacy in spite of these handicaps, the architects adopted the following solution. But for a prescribed minimum 3 ft. setback from the side lines, the house occupies the whole of the site. It is screened against the neighbours by two 18 ft. high redwood screen walls within which the house is developed. To permit the adoption of an open plan, a post-and-beam structural system was used. From the street, precast concrete stepping stones lead under a pergola (which also serves as carport roof) and through an entrance garden with a reflecting pool, to the house entrance. An unobtrusive fence divides the front garden into inner and outer areas. The entrance through the all-glazed facade leads directly in to the living room which, in its front part, extends to the full height of the two-storey building. Adjacent to it, and without physical separation, are kitchen and dining area. The rear side, too, is fully glazed. The upper floor with the two bedrooms and the bathroom is reached via a gently curved staircase which, though in the rear of the house, is visible even from the entrance. The upper floor ends in a balcony above the living room. In the rear of the house, there was still sufficient space for a small garden. Provision has been made for adding further bedrooms above the car port, which would be connected with the balcony by a bridge. Construction: Post-and-beam structure; flat roof and walls of wood. Patio slabs and stepping stones of rough precast concrete.

Haus R. Opdahl in Long Beach, California
Architekten: Edward A. Killingsworth, Jules Brady & Associate

Das Grundstück, das eine Breite von nur 30 Fuß und eine Länge von 80 Fuß (9 × 24 m) hat, liegt sehr beengt in einer Baulücke. Auf beiden Längsseiten rücken ein älteres, zweistöckiges und ein kaum schöneres anderthalbgeschossiges Haus dicht heran. Um dennoch das größtmögliche Maß an Ungestörtheit zu erreichen, kamen die Architekten zu folgender Lösung: Das Haus nutzt die vorhandene Grundfläche voll aus, nur der gesetzlich vorgeschriebene Abstand von der Grundstücksgrenze (3 Fuß) wird eingehalten. 18 Fuß hohe Seitenwände aus Rotholz schirmen gegen die Nachbarn ab, und dazwischen entwickelt sich das Haus, für dessen Skelett – entsprechend dem offenen Grundriß – ein System von Pfosten und Balken verwendet wurde. Von der Straße aus führen vorgefertigte Betonplatten als Trittsteine unter einer Pergola hindurch, die zugleich den Wageneinstellplatz überdacht, zu einem Wassergarten und weiter zur Haustür. Ein leichtes Gitter trennt den Vorgarten in einen inneren und einen äußeren Bereich. Durch den Eingang in der ganz in Glas aufgelösten Frontwand gelangt man direkt in den Wohnraum, der in seinem vorderen Teil durch die volle Höhe des zweigeschossigen Hauses geht. Daran schließen sich ohne Trennung Küche und Eßplatz an. Auch die Rückfront ist ganz verglast. Das obere Stockwerk mit den beiden Schlafräumen und dem Bad erreicht man über eine grazil wirkende, geschwungene Treppe, die, schon vom Eingang her sichtbar, an der Rückwand liegt. Das Obergeschoß endet in einer Galerie über dem Wohnraum. Auf der Rückseite des Hauses hat noch ein kleiner Garten Platz gefunden. Über der Garage sollen später weitere Schlafräume angebaut werden, die von der Galerie aus über eine Brücke erreichbar sind. Konstruktion: Skelett, Flachdach und Wände aus Holz. Terrassen- und Trittsteine aus rauhen vorgefertigten Betonelementen.

3. The pool of water next to the entrance gives the tree-embellished front patio a floating appearance. The reflection in the water provides an optical extension of the patio.

3. Das Wasserbecken neben dem Eingang läßt die baumbestandene Terrasse vor dem Wohnraum als Insel erscheinen, wobei der Spiegeleffekt der Wasserfläche den Hof optisch erweitert.

4. As the front garden is kept dark, the subtle lighting arrangement gives the house, at night, an appearance of greater depth.

5. View from the bedroom balcony through the two-storey glass front on to the inner front garden.

6. Design and materials of the built-in furniture in the open kitchen are so chosen that these fittings appear to be part of the living room. There was thus no need for a physical separation, and the continuity of space is not interrupted.

7. Behind the stairs leading to the upper floor, part of the rear garden can be glimpsed.

8. The 'baroque' effect of the reflection in the pool camouflages the physical boundaries of the house.

4. Da der Vorgarten dunkel gehalten wurde, wirkt das raffiniert beleuchtete Haus bei Nacht tiefer zurückgesetzt.

5. Blick von der Galerie durch die zweigeschossige Glasfront auf den inneren Vorgarten.

6. Die Einbaumöbel der offenen Küche scheinen durch Form und Materialwahl zum Wohnraum zu gehören. So erübrigt sich der Einbau eines Trennelements, und der Raumfluß wird nicht unterbrochen.

7. Hinter der Treppe zum Obergeschoß ist ein Teil des rückseitigen Gartens zu erkennen.

8. Der »barocke« Spiegeleffekt verschleiert die Grenzen des Hauses.

Architect's house at Baden-Baden, Germany
Architect: Egon Eiermann

The site is on a slope north of Baden-Baden, studded with old chestnut, lime and ash trees. The slope falls fairly steeply towards south and less steeply towards west, and because it was proposed to adapt the number of storeys and the roof pitch to those of existing houses in the vicinity, the main building was designed on two floors, the annex on three. The annex, which has a square plan, is set at a bend of the road on the north-western boundary of the site. It contains, from bottom to top, a garage, a studio and drawing office for the owner, and a suite for guests. The main building which is on the upper part of the site also borders on to a road. The main front of this long structure, which has a flat-pitched gable roof, faces the Oos valley in the south-west. The floor levels are adapted to the westwards slope of the ground so that the north-west wing steps down a half-storey in relation to the south-east wing. But as the ridge has been kept at the same level along the entire length of the house, it was possible to make the living-room one-and-a-half storeys high. The differences in level are adjusted by the staircase. The architect's original intention of building a self-contained house for each member of the family is still apparent. In the plan, it can be detected in the row of identical bed-sitting rooms along a side corridor, and in the structural design. The ground floor rooms are so arranged that, if required, the two maids' rooms can be converted into a tenant's flat. The one-and-a-half storey high living room is placed in the north-west wing and is cantilevered so that it partly covers the large garden terrace. Construction: Load bearing cross-walls of brick at 4 metre centres. The cross-walls contain service shafts and support three concrete purlins which carry the wooden rafter construction of the roof. White, asbestos-cement roof without eaves trim or gutter. Ceilings of wood; floors of circular ceramic tiles. Windows without lintels, partly in the form of sliding windows. Under floor heating – embedded hot water pipes.

1. View of the main building from south-west. On the left the north-west wing with terrace and the living room above; on the right the south-east wing. The staggering of the levels is apparent from the different heights of the terraces and balconies. The rain water falling from the roof is intercepted by a gravelfilled trench around the house. In the foreground, part of the small swimming pool is just visible.
2. Main building and annex seen from north-west. There is complete privacy from the road. Brick walls painted dark; white awnings supported by white metal rods; white asbestos-cement roof.

Architektenhaus in Baden-Baden
Architekt: Egon Eiermann

Das Grundstück liegt auf einem Südwesthang im Norden von Baden-Baden. Es ist mit alten Kastanien, Linden und Eschen bewachsen. Die Hangneigung – nach Süden stärker, nach Westen schwächer – und die Absicht, die Gebäudegruppe hinsichtlich der Geschoßzahl und der Dachneigung den Nachbarhäusern anzupassen, machten eine zweigeschossige, beim Nebenhaus sogar dreigeschossige Bebauung notwendig. Das im Grundriß quadratische Nebenhaus ist an eine Straßenkehre an der Nordwestgrenze des Grundstücks gerückt. In ihm sind, von unten nach oben, Garage, Studio und Zeichenraum für den Hausherrn und ein Gästeapartment untergebracht. Das Hauptgebäude auf dem oberen Teil des Grundstücks grenzt gleichfalls an eine Straße. Der langgestreckte Bau mit schwach geneigtem Satteldach wendet sich mit seiner Hauptfront nach Südwesten, zum Oostal. Die Geschosse folgen dem Gefälle des Geländes nach Westen: Der Nordwestflügel ist gegen den Südostflügel um ein halbes Geschoß versetzt. Da über die ganze Hauslänge die gleiche Firsthöhe durchgehalten wurde, konnte der Wohnraum anderthalbgeschossig ausgebildet werden. Der Niveauunterschied wird durch das Treppenhaus ausgeglichen. Die ursprüngliche Idee des Architekten, jedem Familienmitglied ein eigenes, in sich abgeschlossenes Haus zu bauen, ist noch spürbar. Im Grundriß in der Reihung gleicher Wohn-Schlafräume an einem Stichflur und konstruktiv in der Anwendung der Schottenbauweise. Die Räume des Erdgeschosses sind so angeordnet, daß die beiden Mädchenzimmer bei Bedarf in eine Einliegerwohnung verwandelt werden können. Der eineinhalbgeschossige Wohnraum im Nordostflügel überdeckt zum Teil die Gartenterrasse. Konstruktion: Tragende Querwände aus Ziegelmauerwerk, auf denen drei Betonpfetten liegen, die die hölzerne Sparrenkonstruktion tragen. Eternitdach ohne Traufe. Decken Holz, Böden runde Keramikplatten. Sturzlos eingesetzte Fensterelemente, zum Teil als Schiebeflügel ausgebildet. Warmwasser-Fußbodenheizung.

1. Ansicht des Hauptgebäudes von Südwesten. Links der Nordwestflügel mit Terrasse und darüberliegendem Wohnraum, rechts der Südostflügel. Die Geschoßversetzung wird von außen in den verschiedenen Terrassen- und Balkonebenen sichtbar. Das vom Dach herabtropfende Regenwasser fängt eine rings ums Haus geführte Kiesschüttung auf. Im Vordergrund, angeschnitten, das kleine Schwimmbecken.
2. Hauptgebäude und Nebenhaus von Nordwesten. Einblick von der Straße in das Grundstück ist unmöglich. Dunkel gestrichene Backsteinwände; weiße Sonnensegel in weißem Gestänge; weißes Eternitdach.

3. View from south-east of the annex (left) and, on the right, the terrace outside the dining room which, if the curtains are drawn, becomes an enclosed space open merely on top.
4. North-west wing. External floodlights illuminate

the awning and part of the garden, providing an visual extension of the interiors at night.

3. Blick auf das Nebenhaus von Südosten. Rechts die Terrasse vor dem Eßzimmer, die bei

zugezogenen Vorhängen zu einem allseitig umschlossenen, nur nach oben offenen Raum wird.
4. Außenscheinwerfer strahlen die Sonnensegel an und erleuchten teilweise den Garten; die Innenräume werden bei Nacht optisch erweitert.

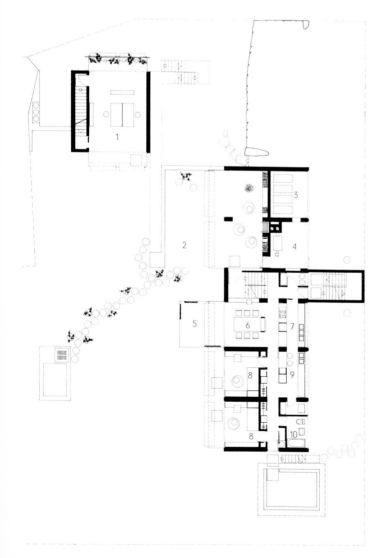
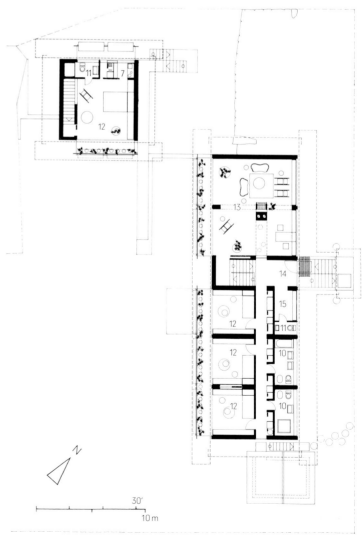

30′
10 m

5. Plans of ground floor (left) and upper floor. Key: 1 studio and drawing office, 2 garden terrace, 3 storage room, 4 boiler room, 5 dining terrace, 6 dining area, 7 kitchen, 8 maid's room, 9 utility room, 10 bathroom, 11 W.C., 12 bed-sitting room, 13 living room, 14 entrance and hall, 15 cloakroom.

6, 7. Like the wall panels, the island type fireplace in the living room is built of dark painted bricks. White concrete slabs, set on edge, but for a narrow opening, enclose the fireplace on both sides and form a recess above the cowl.

8. Working desk in the living room. A white concrete strip at normal storey height connects the fireplace unit with the cross-wall. The space above it corresponds to the additional halfstorey gained by the staggering of levels.

5. Grundrisse von Erdgeschoß (links) und Wohngeschoß. Legende: 1 Studio und Zeichenraum, 2 Gartenterrasse, 3 Vorräte, 4 Heizraum, 5 Eßterrasse, 6 Eßplatz, 7 Küche, 8 Mädchenzimmer, 9 Hauswirtschaftsraum, 10 Bad, 11 WC, 12 Wohn-Schlafraum, 13 Wohnraum, 14 Eingang und Diele, 15 Garderobe.

6, 7. Der frei stehende Kamin des Wohnraums ist wie die Wandscheiben aus Ziegeln gemauert, die dunkel gestrichen sind. Weiße, hochkant gestellte Betonelemente schließen die Feuerstelle nach den Seiten bis auf einen schmalen Schlitz und bilden über der Rauchschürze eine Nische.

8. Blick auf den Arbeitsplatz im Wohnraum. Ein breites Betonband zieht sich in Normalgeschoßhöhe vom Kaminblock zur Querwand. Der Raum darüber entspricht dem durch die Geschoßversetzung gewonnenen zusätzlichen Halbgeschoß.

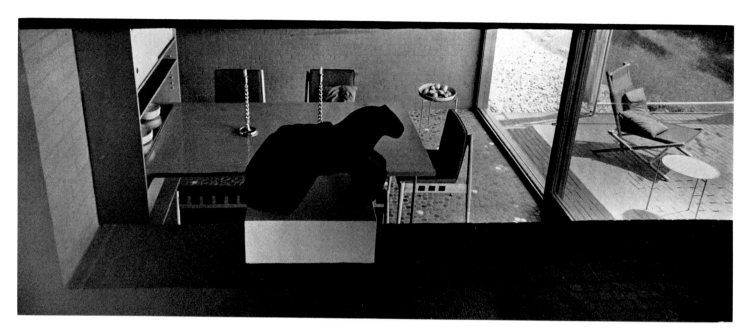

9. The dining room, separated from the kitchen merely by a built-in set of shelves (on the left of the photograph), is connected with the living room by a passage above the stairs.

10. One of the bed-sitting rooms on the main floor. The room is comparatively small (approx. 170 sq. ft.), but there is no need for much furniture as the necessary storage facilities are provided in the corridor. The built-in shelves in the foreground can also serve as table or working top.

11. The roof eaves, project by over 6 ft., and line up with the front edge of the awnings below and with the balcony railings to appear to form a 'second skin'. Alternate panels of the full-height windows can slide sideways in front of the fixed plate glass panels.

12. Annex, seen at night. At ground floor level are studio and drawing office; on the upper floor is the bed-sitting room of the guest suite.

13. The garden, seen from the upper floor of the annex.

9. Das Eßzimmer, das von der Küche nur durch ein Einbauregal (links im Bild) getrennt ist, steht über die Treppe hinweg mit dem Wohnraum in Verbindung.

10. Blick in einen Wohn-Schlafraum des Wohngeschosses. Die Möblierung der rund 16 Quadratmeter großen Zimmer kann sparsam gehalten werden, da der benötigte Schrankraum im Flur untergebracht ist. Im Vordergrund ein eingebautes Regal, das auch als Tisch dient.

11. Die fast zwei Meter vorspringende Dachkante, die damit bündig daruntergespannten Sonnensegel und die Balkongeländer bilden optisch eine zweite Außenhaut der Gebäude. Die raumhohen Fensterelemente sind als seitlich verfahrbare Schiebeflügel ausgebildet, wobei jeweils die Hälfte feststehend angeordnet wurde.

12. Nachtaufnahme des Nebenhauses. Unten Studio und Zeichenraum, oben der Wohn-Schlafraum des Gästeapartments.

13. Blick aus dem Wohngeschoß des Nebenhauses in den Garten.

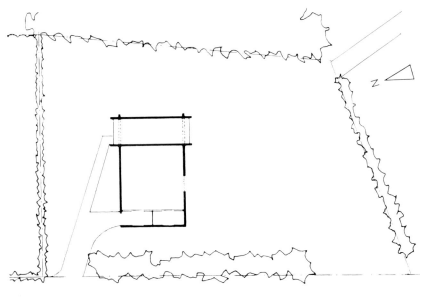

Architect's house at Braband near Aarhus, Denmark
Architects: Knud Friis and Elmar Moltke Nielsen

In the middle of this large site, surrounded by hedges on three sides and bordered by woods on the fourth, the architect used a storey-high brick wall to enclose a self-contained rectangular area. At the western end of this area, Knud Friis placed a single-storey block for garage and workshop, at the other end the two-storey house for his family of four. The ground floor, which from the outside is screened behind the brick wall, is open on the long sides only, facing the courtyard on the west with a wall of glazing and the woods to the east with a strip of waist-high windows. In contrast, the upper floor is open at the ends only whilst the long sides are solid. Quite deliberately, each room is orientated in one direction only although additional light is received through clerestory windows. From the entrance on the north side, one enters through a small lobby with coat cupboard, to the hall where a straight flight of stairs leads to the upper floor. The west wall at the south end of the hall is lined with cupboards. The east side of the ground floor contains the children's bed rooms, bathroom, boiler room, and kitchen with dining area. On the upper floor are study, master bedroom and the living room which enjoys a fine view south over a lake landscape. The study faces north. Construction: Concrete load-bearing walls, which on the outside still bear the marks of the vertical shuttering. Ceiling and flat roof rest on concrete beams.

Architektenhaus in Braband bei Aarhus, Dänemark
Architekten: Knud Friis und Elmar Moltke Nielsen

Aus dem großen Grundstück, das auf drei Seiten von Hecken umgeben ist und auf der vierten Seite an einen Wald angrenzt, schnitt der Architekt Knud Friis mit einer geschoßhohen Ziegelmauer ein Rechteck heraus, in das er an der westlichen Schmalseite einen eingeschossigen Bau für Garage und Werkstatt setzte und auf die gegenüberliegende Seite das zweigeschossige Wohnhaus für die vierköpfige Familie. Das Erdgeschoß, das von außen gesehen hinter der Ziegelmauer verschwindet, ist nur an den Längsseiten geöffnet. Das Obergeschoß ist dagegen nur an den Schmalseiten offen, während die Längsseiten als massive Betonscheiben ausgebildet wurden. Alle Räume sind ganz bewußt nur auf eine Himmelsrichtung orientiert. Vom Eingang auf der Nordseite gelangt man in eine kleine Diele mit Garderobe, an die sich die Halle mit der geradläufigen Treppe zum Obergeschoß anschließt. In ihrer Verlängerung liegt ein großer Schrankraum. Die zweite Längshälfte des Erdgeschosses enthält Bad, Heizraum, Küche mit Eßplatz und Kinderzimmer. Im Obergeschoß liegen Arbeitsraum, Elternschlafzimmer und der Wohnraum, der einen großartigen Ausblick auf eine Seenlandschaft bietet. Das Arbeitszimmer ist nach Norden und der Wohnraum nach Süden orientiert. Konstruktion: Tragende Wände aus Beton, außen als senkrecht geschalter Sichtbeton, Decke und Flachdach auf Betonbalken aufgelegt.

1. The two-storey main building, viewed across the courtyard from the west. The impression of forbidding seclusion created by the upper floor wall is offset by the marks of vertical shuttering left on the untreated concrete and by the strip of clerestory windows between the high, narrow concrete beams.
2. Site plan.
3. The courtyard, surrounded by walls on all sides, has a gate leading to the southern part of the site.
4. South side, the apertures of living room window and courtyard gate form an interesting contrast to the closed wall faces.

1. Blick von Westen über den Innenhof auf das zweigeschossige Wohngebäude. Die vertikale Strukturierung des schalungsrauhen Betons und das Oberlichtband zwischen den schmalen, hohen Betonbalken mildern beim Obergeschoß die abweisende Geschlossenheit.
2. Lageplan.
3. Der allseitig umschlossene Hof öffnet sich durch das Gittertor zum Südteil des Grundstücks.
4. Südansicht. Die Öffnungen von Wohnraumfenster und Gittertor bilden einen spannungsreichen Kontrast zu den geschlossenen Mauerflächen.

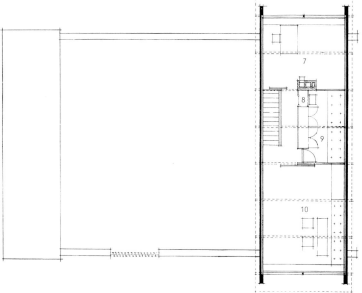

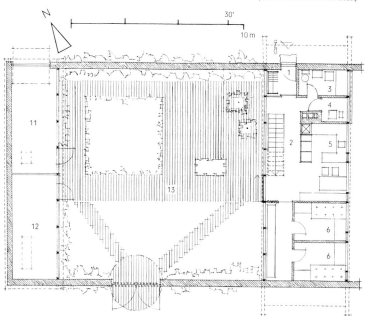

5. Ground floor dining area, with the kitchen on the left.

6. Ground floor hall with the wooden stairs leading to the upper floor. In the background, the western end of the courtyard is marked by the workshop building. To reduce noise, the stairs are raised above the floor by means of flat irons. The handrail is not fixed to the stairs but suspended from the upper floor balustrade.

7. Upper floor corridor with entrance and study. Next to the glass sliding door of the latter is the hatch of the kitchen lift.

8. Plans of upper floor and ground floor (bottom). Key: 1 entrance, 2 hall with stairs, 3 bathroom and W.C., 4 boiler room, 5 kitchen with dining area, 6 children's room, 7 study, 8 kitchen lift, 9 master bedroom, 10 living room, 11 garage, 12 workshop, 13 courtyard.

5. Eßplatz im Erdgeschoß, links davon schließt die Küche an.

6. Die Halle im Erdgeschoß mit der Holztreppe zum Obergeschoß. Als westlicher Abschluß des Innenhofes ist im Hintergrund die Werkstatt zu erkennen. Um eine Übertragung des Trittschalls zu vermeiden, wurde die Treppe mit Flacheisen vom Boden abgehoben; der Handlauf ist nicht an der Treppe befestigt, sondern vom Geländer des Obergeschosses abgehängt.

7. Blick vom Flur des Obergeschosses auf Eingang und Arbeitsraum, neben dessen Glasschiebetür die Klappe des Speisenaufzugs zu erkennen ist, der zur Küche hinunterführt.

8. Grundrisse von Obergeschoß und Erdgeschoß (unten). Legende: 1 Eingang, 2 Treppenhalle, 3 Bad und WC, 4 Heizraum, 5 Küche mit Eßplatz, 6 Kinderzimmer, 7 Arbeitsraum, 8 Speisenaufzug, 9 Elternschlafraum, 10 Wohnraum, 11 Garage, 12 Werkstatt, 13 Gartenhof.

9, 10. In the living room, the materials of walls and ceiling come fully into their own.

9, 10. Im Wohnraum kommt das Material von Wänden und Decke in seiner natürlichen Struktur und Form voll zur Geltung.

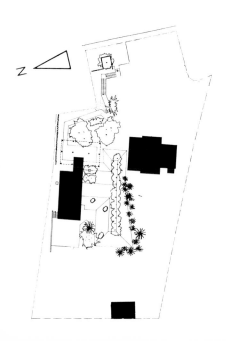

House on the Coastal Road, Klampenborg, Denmark
Architect: Erik Christian Sørensen

This house, built for a family of five, was erected in the garden of a 19th-century villa, on a sloping site to the north of Copenhagen with a view across the Sound towards the Swedish coast. As the view is towards the east and the old house only a few yards from the south side of the site, the living room wing has been designed to face east and west. In addition the design had to be adapted to the contours of an old fortification mound which cuts across the site.

The house consists of two wings, placed at right angles, staggered in height and connected by a staircase. The east wing comprising living room and kitchen, is set on stilts. The west, bedroom wing rests on the load-bearing walls of the lower floor. A zigzag path leads from the east side of the site to the entrance in the open ground floor of the living room wing. One flight of stairs connects the entrance with the upper floor of the bedroom wing, another leads to the living room wing where the hall gives access to the living room proper and to the kitchen. The living room is divided into three sections; the southern part, extending over the entire width of the house, has two west windows to admit the afternoon sun; the central part is focused on the fireplace; the third serves as dining area. With this arrangement, it is possible to have a full view of the room yet, by appropriate arrangement of the furniture, to create intimate zones. On the upper floor of the two-storey west wing are the parents' and children's bedrooms and a large playroom. On the lower floor are utility rooms, the maid's room and a hobby room. Construction: Load bearing walls and supporting frame of reinforced concrete. Roof of lightweight concrete ('Siporex') in several layers. Wall panels of concrete sprayed on to wire mesh, insulated with 'Styropor' and lined internally with gypsum boards faced with canvas. Floors are concrete slabs finished with teak blocks on the upper floors, and tiles in the basement. Ceilings clad in oregon pine boarding. Oil-fired hot water central heating.

1. View from the east, showing the window wall of the living room wing. This rather unobtrusive facade is subtly textured by its combination of functional elements, (from top to bottom) ventilation flaps, square glass panels, (either fixed or sliding), inclined ventilation grilles hiding 'the convectors, glazing strip.
2. Site plan.
3. Living room wing, seen from the south. Apart from the high level clerestory window the south side is closed. Between the framing posts are solid, white-painted concrete panels.
4. North-east corner of the house. In the background, the free-standing chimney.

1. Blick von Osten auf die Fensterfront des Wohnteils. Die zurückhaltend wirkende Fassade zeigt eine sensible Gliederung, die sich aus der Kombination der funktional bedingten Fassadenelemente ergibt (von oben nach unten): Lüftungsflügel, quadratische Scheiben (feststehend oder als Schiebefenster), Brüstung mit schrägliegenden Lüftungslamellen, dahinter die Konvektoren, Glasstreifen.
2. Lageplan.
3. Der Wohnflügel von Süden gesehen. Die Südseite ist bis auf das hochliegende Fensterband geschlossen. Zwischen den Wandstützen die weiß gestrichenen, massiven Betonpanels.
4. Die Nordostecke des Hauses. Im Hintergrund der frei stehende Schornstein.

Haus am Strandvej in Klampenborg, Dänemark
Architekt: Erik Christian Sørensen

Das für eine fünfköpfige Familie erbaute Haus steht auf einem Hanggrundstück nördlich von Kopenhagen mit Blick über den Öresund zur schwedischen Küste. Es wurde im Garten einer Villa aus dem 19. Jahrhundert errichtet. Da die Aussicht nach Osten geht und der Abstand zu dem alten Haus auf der Südseite des Areals nur wenige Meter beträgt, ist der Wohnflügel nach Osten und Westen orientiert. Außerdem wurde die Form des Gebäudes den Konturen des alten Festungswalls angepaßt, der durch das Grundstück verläuft. – Das Haus besteht aus zwei zueinander quergestellten und gegeneinander in der Höhe versetzten Blöcken, die durch das Treppenhaus miteinander verbunden sind. Der Ostflügel, der den Wohnraum und die Küche umfaßt, steht auf Stützen. Der rechtwinklig anschließende Westflügel mit den Schlafräumen ruht auf einem Untergeschoß mit massiven Wandscheiben. Ein im Zickzack angelegter Weg führt von der Ostseite des Grundstücks zum Eingang im offenen Stützengeschoß unter dem Wohnflügel. Von hier aus gelangt man über wenige Stufen hinunter zum Untergeschoß unter dem Schlafteil. Eine Treppe verbindet den Eingang mit dem höherliegenden Hauptgeschoß dieses Flügels. Ein weiterer Treppenlauf führt von hier aus hinauf in den Wohnteil, wo eine Diele den Wohnbereich und die Küche erschließt. Der Wohnraum ist dreifach unterteilt: der über die ganze Hausbreite reichende südliche Teil hat nach Westen zwei Fenster, um die Nachmittagssonne hereinzulassen, der mittlere Teil ist dem Kamin zugeordnet und der dritte dient als Eßplatz. Durch diese Aufteilung ist es möglich, den Raum in seiner ganzen Größe zu überblicken und doch durch entsprechende Anordnung der Möbel intime Bereiche zu schaffen. Der zweigeschossige Westflügel enthält im Obergeschoß die Schlafräume der Eltern und der Kinder und ein großes Spielzimmer. Im Untergeschoß befinden sich Wirtschaftsräume, das Mädchenzimmer und ein Hobbyraum. Konstruktion: Tragende Wände und Stützrahmen aus Stahlbeton. Dach aus Siporex-Platten mit mehrschichtiger Auflage. Fußböden aus Betonteilen, im Untergeschoß mit Fliesen, in den oberen Geschossen mit Teakholz belegt. Deckenverkleidung aus Oregon Pine. Ölgefeuerte Warmwasser-Zentralheizung.

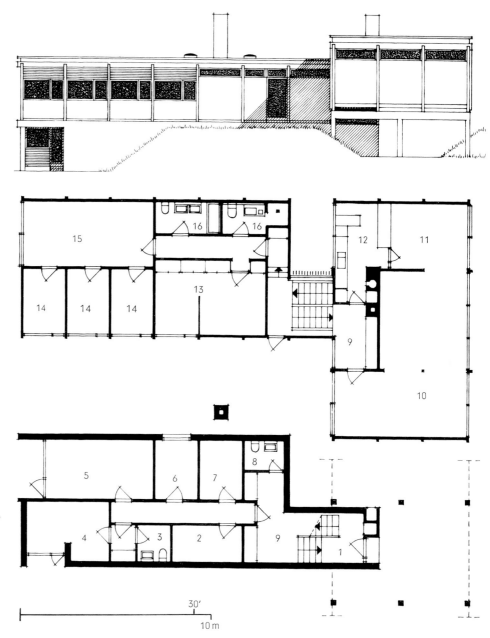

5. Since only part of the west wing cuts into the old mound, it was possible to gain space in the basement for two habitable rooms, a maid's room and a hobby room.

6. Entrance zone, with the black-painted concrete columns below the living room wing.

7. Entrance with the staircase which links the two parts of the building.

8. South elevation and plans of upper floor (centre) and lower floor (bottom). Key: 1 entrance, 2 store room, 3 bathroom, 4 maid's room, 5 hobby room, 6 laundry, 7 boiler room, 8 W.C., 9 hall, 10 living room, 11 dining area, 12 kitchen with breakfast room, 13 master bedroom with dressing room, 14 children's room, 15 children's play room, 16 bathroom and W.C.

9. South side. Apart from the narrow top strip window, the south side of the rooms is completely closed as the old villa is only a few yards away.

10. Towards the western end, the two storeys of the bedroom wing become fully visible.

5. Da der Westflügel nur zum Teil in den alten Wall einschneidet, war es möglich, im Untergeschoß zwei bewohnbare Räume – Mädchenzimmer und Hobbyraum – zu gewinnen.

6. Der Eingangsbereich mit den schwarz gestrichenen Betonstützen unter dem Wohnflügel.

7. Eingang und Treppenhaus, das als Gelenk die beiden Baukörper verbindet.

8. Ansicht der Südseite und Grundrisse von Obergeschoß (Mitte) und Untergeschoß (unten). Legende: 1 Eingang, 2 Vorratsraum, 3 Bad, 4 Mädchenzimmer, 5 Hobbyraum, 6 Waschküche, 7 Heizraum, 8 WC, 9 Diele, 10 Wohnraum, 11 Eßplatz, 12 Küche mit Frühstücksplatz, 13 Elternschlafraum mit Ankleide, 14 Kinderzimmer, 15 Kinderspielzimmer, 16 Bad und WC.

9. Südansicht. Bis auf ein schmales Oberlichtband sind die Räume nach Süden vollkommen geschlossen, da nur wenige Meter entfernt das alte Haus steht.

10. Gegen Westen werden beide Geschosse des Schlafteils voll sichtbar.

11. Living room. In the foreground left is the fireplace wall, in the background the dining area. Teak block flooring; ceiling clad in oregon pine boarding.

12. The wall beside the fireplace is faced with blue glazed ceramic tiles.

13. Kitchen with breakfast area. The shelves of the built-in cupboards, including those on the window side (left) are within easy reach. On the right, the glazed toplight overlooking the dining area.

11. Blick in den Wohnraum. Im Vordergrund links die Kaminwand, im Hintergrund der Eßplatz. Fußboden Teakholzparkett, Deckenschalung Oregon Pine.

12. Der Wandstreifen neben der Feueröffnung des Kamins ist mit blauen, glasierten Keramikplatten verkleidet.

13. Küche mit Frühstücksplatz und den in Greifhöhe eingebauten Wandschränken, auch in der Fensterwand links. Rechts das Oberlichtband zum Eßplatz.

14, 15. The children's bedrooms open into their playroom (Fig. 15).

14, 15. Das Spielzimmer (Bild 15) der Kinder liegt vor den Kinderschlafzimmern.

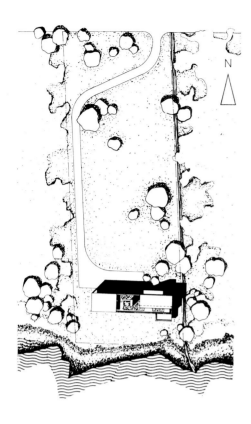

House for W. J. Merz at Môtier, Murtensee, Switzerland
Architects: Studio 5

The rectangular site on the north shore of Murtensee slopes gently down from the access road to the lake. As the owner wanted all the rooms to face the lake, the resulting house was a long, narrow building extending over nearly the whole width of the site. Because of the risk of flooding, and to ensure an unimpeded view from the main floor across the reeds and shrubs to the lake, the house has been set on stilts. Because of the high ground water level, no basement was provided. On the north side, away from the lake, the building is almost completely closed in; but it is opened up by the different window openings and the concrete frame of the double-height covered terrace on the west side. The projecting staircase which, as it were, extends the ground floor aperture upwards, forms a markedly plastic accent. From the approach road on the west side, the lake shore is clearly visible through the ground floor porch. The space between the stanchions serves as a car port. The technical installations are concentrated in the enclosed part of the ground floor. On the main floor, living room and bedrooms are separated by kitchen, bathroom and W.C., and are connected by a corridor parallel to the stairs. On the partly roofed top floor are a guest room, the maid's room, and a roof garden where a canopied sitting space is connected by stairs with the main floor terrace. A second flight of outside stairs on the west side links the covered terrace with the garden. Built into the fireplace unit is a food lift to the roof garden operated from the dining room. All the rooms face south, and the only large window on the north side is that of the dining room. The terrace is connected with the bedroom balcony by a covered gallery which runs along the entire south side and serves as sun and weather protection. Construction: Reinforced concrete framework on piles of 6 metres (20 ft) depth. The north and east sides are solid concrete walls. Thermal insulation is provided by 'Duplex' boards (foamed plastic with gypsum). Inside rendering of white lime plaster. Roof lined with mastic asphalt and covered by a 20 cm (8″) thick layer of earth. Sliding windows in aluminium frames. Oil-fired central heating.

1. North side, with the lake in the background.
2. South side of the house, seen from the lake.
3. Site plan.
4. General view from north-east.

1. Die Nordseite, dahinter der Murtensee.
2. Die zum See orientierte Südseite.
3. Lageplan.
4. Gesamtansicht von Nordosten.

Haus W. J. Merz in Môtier am Murtensee, Schweiz
Architekten: Atelier 5

Das langgestreckte Grundstück am Nordufer des Murtensees fällt von der Zufahrtsstraße flach zum Seeufer ab. Da auf Wunsch des Bauherrn sämtliche Räume seewärts zu orientieren waren, ergab sich ein schmaler rechteckiger Baukörper, der fast die ganze Grundstücksbreite einnimmt. Wegen der Überschwemmungsgefahr steht das Gebäude auf Stützen. Zudem bietet sich von dem angehobenen Wohngeschoß aus ein unbehinderter Seeblick über Schilf und Büsche hinweg. Der hohe Grundwasserspiegel ließ von einer Unterkellerung absehen. Nach Norden, zur Landseite hin, ist der kantige Baublock fast völlig geschlossen. Eine Auflockerung bringen die verschiedenen Fensteröffnungen und der Betonrahmen um die doppelgeschossige Wohnterrasse auf der Westseite. Das vorgesetzte Treppenhaus, das die Öffnung des Erdgeschosses nach oben führt, bildet einen starken plastischen Akzent. Von der Zufahrt auf der Westseite des Grundstücks aus hat man einen freien Blick durch die Erdgeschoßhalle auf das Seeufer. Der Raum zwischen den Stützen dient als Wageneinstellplatz. Im ummauerten Teil des Erdgeschosses sind technische Räume untergebracht. Im Hauptgeschoß werden Wohn- und Schlafbereich durch die Naßräume Küche, Bad und WC getrennt. Ein Flur parallel zur Treppe verbindet die beiden Teile. Das Dachgeschoß umfaßt Gast- und Mädchenzimmer sowie einen Dachgarten, von dessen überdecktem Sitzplatz eine Treppe zur Terrasse des Hauptgeschosses hinunterführt. Eine zweite, außenliegende Treppe an der Westseite verbindet die Wohnterrasse mit dem Garten. In den Kaminblock wurde ein vom Eßzimmer aus zu bedienender Speisenaufzug zum Dachgarten eingebaut. Alle Räume sind nach Süden geöffnet, nur das Eßzimmer hat ein größeres Nordfenster. Die Wohnterrasse ist mit dem Balkon vor dem Schlafzimmer durch einen gedeckten Laufgang verbunden, der sich die ganze Südfront entlangzieht. Er dient zugleich als Sonnen- und Wetterschutz. Konstruktion: Stahlbetonskelett auf 6 m tief reichendem Pfahlfundament. Nord- und Ostfassade als Scheiben betoniert. Wärmeisolation mit Duplexplatten (Kunststoffschaum-Gips), innen mit weißem Kalkmörtel verputzt. Dach mit Isolierung aus Gußasphalt, darüber eine 20 cm starke Humusschicht. Schiebefenster in Aluminiumrahmen. Ölzentralheizung.

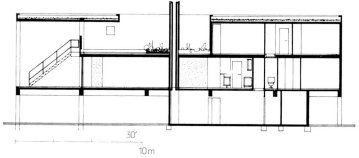

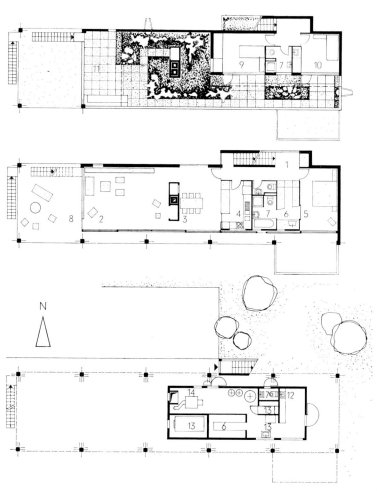

5. The staircase projecting from the north side. Its function is clearly revealed by its outlines and apertures.
6. Longitudinal section and (from the bottom to top) ground floor plan, first floor plan and roof storey plan. Key: 1 entrance and hall, 2 living room, 3 dining area, 4 kitchen, 5 bedroom, 6 dressing room, 7 bathroom, shower bath and W.C., 8 covered terrace, 9 guest room, 10 maid's room, 11 roof garden, 12 workshop, 13 cellar, 14 boiler room.

5. Das vor die Nordfassade gezogene Treppenhaus, dessen Funktion von außen an den Konturen und den Lichtöffnungen klar ablesbar ist.
6. Längsschnitt und Grundrisse. Von unten nach oben: Erdgeschoß, erstes Obergeschoß, Dachgeschoß. Legende: 1 Eingang und Diele, 2 Wohnraum, 3 Eßplatz, 4 Küche, 5 Schlafraum, 6 Schrankraum, 7 Bad, Dusche und WC, 8 Gedeckte Terrasse, 9 Gastzimmer, 10 Mädchenzimmer, 11 Dachgarten, 12 Werkstatt, 13 Kellerräume, 14 Heizraum.

7. Dining area and bedroom corridor, seen from the living room. The doors extend to the continuous ceiling. Flooring of precast concrete tiles.
8. The dining area backs on to the fireplace unit.
9, 10. The appearance of the living room is dominated by the fully glazed south front and the black slate face of the fireplace unit. Because of

the sliding windows, the rooms can be opened-out towards the lake.

7. Blick vom Wohnbereich über Eßplatz und Flur zum Schlafraum. Durchgehende Decke, raumhohe Türen. Fußboden vorfabrizierte Waschbetonplatten.

8. Der Eßplatz ist an die Rückwand des Kaminblocks gerückt.
9, 10. Der Raumeindruck des Wohnbereiches wird beherrscht durch die voll verglaste Südwand und den mit schwarzen Schieferplatten verkleideten Kaminblock. Die Schiebefenster öffnen die Räume zum See.

11. Roof garden with covered sitting space. The combination of the light-coloured rough concrete facings and the concrete floor slabs has been consistently adhered to.

12. The cantilevered roof slab above the partly covered top storey provides adequate weather and sun protection for guest room and maid's room which, like the rooms on the main floor, have room-high windows facing the lake.

13. Double-height covered terrace outside the living room. The extension of the roof slab also protects the sitting space on the roof garden which is reached by a straight flight of stairs.

14. Covered gallery along the south side, with the bedroom balcony in the background. Access of light and sun is regulated by sun blinds placed between the stanchions close to the front edge of the projecting roof.

15. North-east corner with its enclosing rough concrete walls and eaves overhanging the roof garden.

11. Der Dachgarten mit dem überdeckten Sitzplatz. Die Materialeinheit des hellen Sichtbetons und der Waschbeton-Bodenplatten ist bis ins Detail konsequent durchgehalten.

12. Im Dachgeschoß bietet die auskragende Deckenplatte ausreichenden Wetter- und Sonnenschutz für Gast- und Mädchenzimmer, die wie die Räume des Hauptgeschosses zum See hin wandhoch verglast sind.

13. Die zwei Geschosse hohe Terrasse vor dem Wohnraum. Die Verlängerung ihrer Deckenplatte überdacht zugleich den Sitzplatz des Dachgartens, zu dem eine geradläufige Treppe führt.

14. Der gedeckte Laufgang vor der Südfront, im Hintergrund der Schlafzimmerbalkon. Lamellenstores, die zwischen den Stützen hinter der Deckenvorderkante angebracht sind, regulieren den Licht- und Sonneneinfall.

15. Die geschlossenen, schalungsrauh belassenen Sichtbetonflächen der Nordostecke mit der Traufe des Dachgartens.

Architect's house and a companion house in Cambridge, England
Architect: Colin St. John Wilson

The two houses are erected on two adjacent 50 × 150 ft. plots with east-west orientation. Seen from the road, these two-storey houses appear to be one. Yet, as the plan shows, the houses are staggered: the house to the north, occupied by the architect himself, has an entrance courtyard outside the living area, flanked on the road side by an L-shaped first floor studio. The living rooms are on the west side; but patios are provided in both houses to give the living rooms a southern aspect as well. In both houses the arrangement of the rooms is very similar. Entrances and staircases are at the intersection of the two wings. Straight ahead from the entrance, one enters the living room; on the left are dining room and kitchen. On the upper floors are the bedrooms and bathrooms, accessible from short corridors. The studio section in the architect's own house is set over the covered way and the garage and reached from a separate staircase. Both houses have a common module and structural system. Construction: combination of bearing walls and concrete block columns. Walls are fair-faced blockwork both inside and out, except in bedrooms and bathrooms which are plastered. Floors are tiled in white rubber. Electric underfloor heating.

Architektenhaus in Cambridge, England
Architekt: Colin St. John Wilson

Zu überbauen waren zwei nebeneinanderliegende schmale Grundstücke von rund 15 × 45 m Größe, die von Osten nach Westen verlaufen. In der Straßenansicht erscheinen die zweigeschossigen Häuser als ein einziger langgestreckter Block. Wie der Grundriß zeigt, sind die Baukörper jedoch gegeneinander versetzt: bei dem nördlich gelegenen Haus, das der Architekt selbst bewohnt, ist dem Wohnteil ein Eingangshof vorgelagert, um den sich ein L-förmiger Bürotrakt gruppiert. Um den nach Westen gelegenen Wohnraum auch von Süden belichten zu können, sind beide Häuser winkelförmig angelegt. Raumanordnung und -abfolge entsprechen sich weitgehend. Im Schnittpunkt der beiden Schenkel liegen Eingang und Treppe zum Obergeschoß. Geradeaus gelangt man in den Wohnraum, links durch das Eßzimmer in die Küche. Die Flügel umschließen jeweils einen Gartenhof. In den Obergeschossen sind, über Stichflure zugänglich, Schlafräume und Bäder untergebracht. Die beiden Zeichen- und Büroräume im Haus des Architekten, die über dem offenen Durchgang und der Garage liegen, werden über ein eigenes Treppenhaus erschlossen. Beide Häuser sind nach dem gleichen Modul und dem gleichen Konstruktionssystem errichtet. Konstruktion: Kombination von tragenden Wänden und Stützen aus Zementblocksteinen. Wände außen und innen, mit Ausnahme der Schlafräume und Bäder, unverputzt. Fußbodenbelag weiße Kautschukfliesen. Elektrische Fußbodenheizung.

1. West side with paved patio and the living room frontage of the architect's own house. On the right, partly hidden by the high wall and the sculpture by Paolozzi, is the second house. The elevation is dominated by the motif of the concrete block columns.
2, 3. View from the east. The houses are separated from the road by a front garden and a low wooden fence. The ground floor facade is arcaded whilst the seclusion of the upper floor frontage is only broken by a few small windows. The contrast between the two storeys is emphasized by the open passage to the entrance courtyard of the architect's own house. On the north and south sides are solid walls.

1. Blick von Westen auf den Gartenhof und die Wohnraumfront des Architektenhauses. Rechts, teilweise durch die geschoßhohe Mauer und die Plastik von Paolozzi verdeckt, das zweite Haus. Der Aufriß wird durch das Motiv der gemauerten Stütze bestimmt.
2, 3. Ansicht von Osten. Vorgarten und Holzplanke trennen die Häuser von der Straße. Die Fassade des Erdgeschosses ist in Stützen aufgelöst, darüber der geschlossene Block des Obergeschosses, nur von wenigen kleinen Fenstern durchbrochen. Der Kontrast zwischen den beiden Geschossen wird verstärkt durch den offenen Durchgang zum Eingangshof des Architektenhauses. Nord- und Südfassade sind als massive Wandscheiben ausgebildet.

4. All the interior views are of the architect's own house. This is a view of the entrance hall with the stairs leading to the upper floor. Top lighting. The gallery leads to bedrooms and library.

4. Alle Innenaufnahmen stammen aus dem Haus des Architekten. Blick in die Eingangshalle mit der Treppe zum Obergeschoß. Die Belichtung erfolgt durch Oberlichter. Über die Galerie erreicht man Schlafräume und Bibliothek.

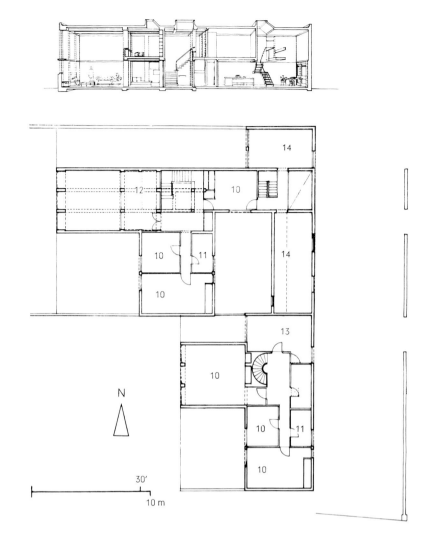

N

30'

10 m

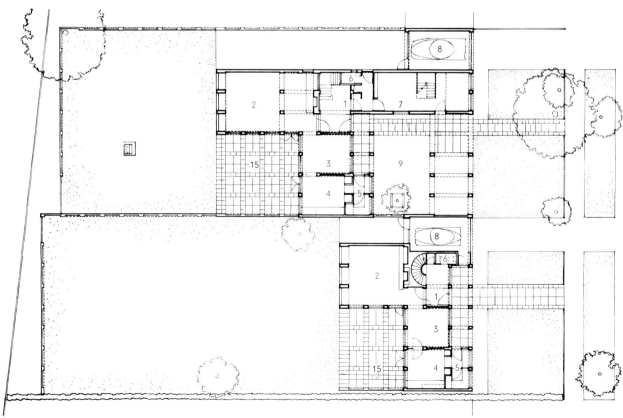

5. Section and plans of ground floor (bottom) and upper floor. Key: 1 entrance hall, 2 living room, 3 dining room, 4 kitchen, 5 larder, 6 W.C., 7 office, 8 garage, 9 entrance courtyard, 10 bedroom, 11 bathroom, 12 gallery and library, 13 studio, 14 drawing office, 15 walled garden.
6. Two-storey living room, with gallery and library. In the background on the right is the door to the entrance hall, next to it the passage to the dining room and the door to the walled garden. Daylight conditions in the library are improved by top lighting. Below the gallery is the fireside sitting area.
7. The juxtaposition of untreated walls, columns and concrete beams with plastered ceiling panels and white floor tiles has a restful overall effect. The windows have blinds instead of curtains.
8. Kitchen, seen from the dining-room.

5. Schnitt und Grundrisse von Erdgeschoß (unten) und Obergeschoß. Legende: 1 Eingangshalle, 2 Wohnraum, 3 Eßzimmer, 4 Küche, 5 Speisekammer, 6 WC, 7 Büro, 8 Garage, 9 Eingangshof, 10 Schlafraum, 11 Bad, 12 Galerie und Bibliothek, 13 Studio, 14 Büro und Zeichenraum, 15 Gartenhof.
6. Der zweigeschossige Wohnraum mit Blick auf Galerie und Bibliothek. Rechts im Hintergrund die Tür zur Eingangshalle, daneben Durchgang zum Eßzimmer und Tür zum Gartenhof. Die Bibliothek erhält zusätzliches Tageslicht durch Oberlichter. Unter der Galerie der Kaminsitzplatz.
7. Die roh belassenen Wände, Stützen und Betontragbalken ergeben zusammen mit den glatt verputzten weißen Deckenfeldern und den ebenfalls weißen Fliesen des Bodenbelags eine harmonische Gesamtwirkung. Die Fenster haben an Stelle von Vorhängen Rollos.
8. Blick vom Eßzimmer in die Küche.

House for A. McCracken, Port Murray near Maidens, Ayrshire, Scotland
Architect: Peter Womersley

1. View from the south. The large sundeck and the main entrance. Because of the stagger of the two parts of the house, it was possible to create an outdoor sitting area protected on the north side.
2. View from the north. Living room and balcony project over the walled lower floor. In the centre of the picture is the high-ceilinged dining room, next to it the kitchen balcony. The deep cross-member of the dining room window forms visual extension of the living room floor slab.
3. The house seen from a distance at low tide.

1. Blick von Süden auf die große Sonnenterrasse und den Haupteingang. Durch die Versetzung der beiden Baukörper konnte ein gegen Norden geschützter Freisitzplatz geschaffen werden.
2. Blick von Norden. Wohnraum und Balkon kragen über das gemauerte Untergeschoß aus. In der Bildmitte der hohe Eßraum, daran anschließend die Küchenveranda. Die breite Quersprosse des Eßzimmerfensters setzt optisch die Bodenplatte des Wohnraumes fort.
3. Gesamtansicht des Hauses bei Ebbe.

This house, owned by the building contractor himself, was erected at the edge of the site which is a rocky peninsula. The beach, where a boat house and jetty are still to be built, is within easy reach. The building consists of two parts staggered in relation to each other and connected by the double height hall/dining room. As the ground slopes down to the beach, the wing facing the sea has a lower floor, where the windows are deliberately kept small and unobtrusive so as not to distract from the 'block' effect of the building as a whole. The upper floor on this side is slightly raised above the wing on the inland side. The house is thus developed on three levels, staggered by the height of half a storey. In the recessed lower floor of the two-storey wing are master bedroom, bathroom and guest room, in the overhanging upper floor a study and a living room which opens on to a balcony with glass sides and parapet. From the living room level, a few steps lead down to the dining room and thence to the third level on the lower floor. The dining room floor is level with that of the single-storey wing, whilst its ceiling is level with that of the upper floor of the two-storey wing. In the single-storey wing, kitchen, shower bath and three children's bedrooms are arranged along a cupboarded corridor which also leads to the garage. The children's bedrooms and the kitchen, overlook a porch which widens into a balcony and projects to give a view of the sea and bathing beach. The house is designed primarily for holidays and weekends. Construction: Lower floor: rubble walling. Upper storeys: white-painted, timber frame structure resting on reinforced concrete slabs with posts at 6 ft. centres; windows alternate with panels of diagonally braced horizontal boarding. Timber roof. Electric floor heating.

Haus A. McCracken, Port Murray bei Maidens in Ayrshire, Schottland
Architekt: Peter Womersley

Dieses Haus eines Bauunternehmers wurde am Rande des Grundstückes, einer felsigen Landzunge, errichtet. So kann man auf kürzestem Wege den Strand erreichen, wo noch ein Bootshaus und ein Anlegesteg gebaut werden sollen. Das Gebäude besteht aus zwei gegeneinander versetzten Baukörpern, die durch den anderthalb Geschosse hohen Eßraum miteinander verbunden sind. Da das Gelände zum Strand hin abfällt, ergab sich unter dem zum Meer vorgeschobenen Flügel ein Untergeschoß, dessen Fenster klein und unbetont gelassen wurden, um die blockhafte Wirkung nicht zu stören; das darüberliegende Obergeschoß wurde gegenüber dem landeinwärts liegenden Trakt leicht angehoben. Das Haus entwickelt sich also auf drei halbgeschossig versetzten Ebenen. Der zweigeschossige Teil enthält im zurückgesetzten Untergeschoß Elternschlafraum, Bad und Gästezimmer, im auskragenden Obergeschoß Studio und Wohnraum, vor dessen Stirnseite ein Balkon mit verglasten Seitenwänden und Glasbrüstungen liegt. Von der Wohnebene führen einige Stufen hinab zum Eßzimmer und von dort hinunter auf die dritte Ebene im Untergeschoß. Der Fußboden des Eßzimmers ist niveaugleich mit dem Boden des eingeschossigen Flügels, die Decke ist jedoch eine Fortführung des zweigeschossigen Traktes. Im eingeschossigen Flügel sind Küche, Duschraum und drei Kinderzimmer an einem langen Schrankflur aufgereiht, der zugleich Garage und Eingangsdiele verbindet. Von den Schlafkojen der Kinder aus und von der Küche kann man direkt auf eine Veranda treten, die sich vor der Küche zu einem Balkon verbreitert. Das Haus wird in erster Linie für Ferien- und Wochenendaufenthalte verwendet. Konstruktion: Untergeschoß aus Bruchsteinmauerwerk. Obergeschosse in weiß gestrichener Holzrahmenkonstruktion auf Betonplatte, Achsabstand 6 Fuß; an den Außenwänden Wechsel von verglasten und holzverschalten, diagonal versteiften Wandfeldern. Dach Holzkonstruktion. Elektrische Fußbodenheizung.

96

4. Site plan.
5. Longitudinal section and plans of lower floor (bottom) and upper floor. Key: 1 entrance and hall, 2 study, 3 living room, 4 dining room, 5 kitchen, 6 shower bath and W.C., 7 children's bedrooms, 8 garage, 9 balcony, 10 master bedroom, 11 bathroom and W.C., 12 guest room.
6. The floor of the balcony in front of the children's rooms and kitchen is of Sicilian marble.

4. Lageplan.
5. Längsschnitt und Grundrisse von Untergeschoß (unten) und Obergeschoß. Legende: 1 Eingang und Diele, 2 Studio, 3 Wohnraum, 4 Eßzimmer, 5 Küche, 6 Dusche und WC, 7 Kinderzimmer, 8 Garage, 9 Balkon, 10 Elternschlafzimmer, 11 Bad und WC, 12 Gästezimmer.
6. Die Veranda vor Kinderzimmer und Küche hat einen Plattenboden aus sizilianischem Marmor.

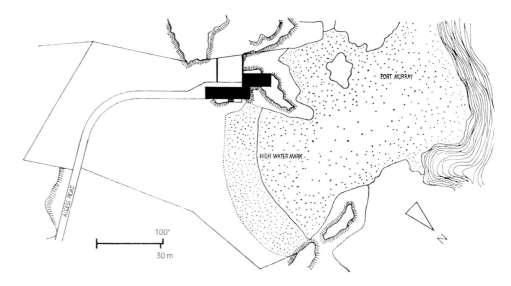
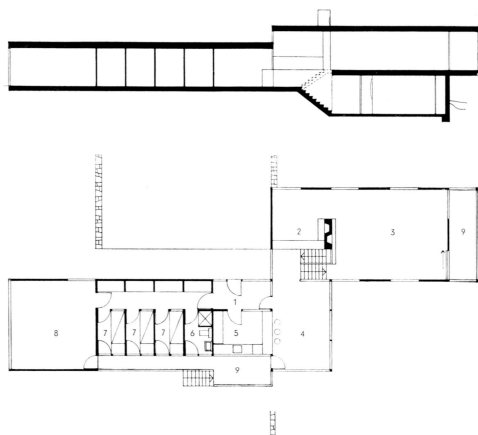
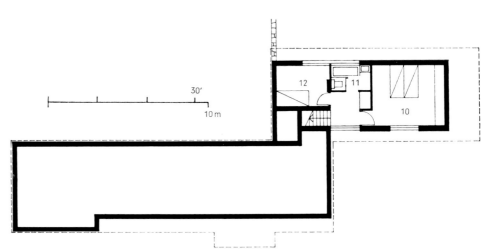

7. From the kitchen balcony, steps lead down to the beach.

8. The two-storey wing, seen from the south. The lower floor windows are those of bathroom and guest room.

9. The large hatch between kitchen and dining area can be closed by glass sliding doors.

7. Von der Küchenveranda führt eine Treppe zum Strand.

8. Ansicht des zweigeschossigen Traktes von Süden. Im Sockel die Fenster von Bad und Gästezimmer.

9. Die große Durchreiche zwischen der Küche und dem Eßplatz läßt sich durch Glasschiebetüren schließen.

10. Dining room, seen from the study, with the kitchen hatch on the right. Floor of white marble. Walls panelled with teak and cypress boarding, or plastered and painted white.

11. Intersection of the three levels at the dining room. The steps lead up to the living room. Behind them is the passage to the lower floor. Behind the balustrade is the study. The rooms interlink yet are clearly defined.

12. Living room with fireplace, with the study in the background. On the left are the steps to the dining room, in the background, the glass door leading to the hall. The mantleshelf is of black Belgian marble, the fireplace itself of white Sicilian marble.

13. Living room, seen from the study. Large floor to ceiling windows provide a view on three sides. When the glass sliding doors are open, the balcony forms part of the living room.

10. Blick vom Studio in das Eßzimmer, rechts die Durchreiche. Der Boden ist mit weißen Marmorplatten belegt. Für die Wandverkleidung wurde Zypressen- und Teakholz verwendet. Die Wände sind weiß belassen.

11. Schnittpunkt der drei Wohnebenen im Eßzimmer. Die Treppe führt in den Wohnraum. Dahinter der Abgang zum Untergeschoß. Hinter der Brüstung das Studio. Die Räume durchdringen sich und sind doch deutlich gegeneinander abgesetzt.

12. Der Wohnraum mit Kamin und dahinter liegendem Studio. Links der Abgang zum Eßzimmer und im Hintergrund die Glastür zur Eingangsdiele. Die Kaminkonsole besteht aus schwarzem belgischem Marmor, der Kamin selbst aus weißem sizilianischem Marmor.

13. Ansicht des Wohnraums vom Studio her. Große, wandhohe Fenster geben den Blick nach drei Seiten frei. Bei geöffneten Glasschiebetüren bildet der Balkon einen Teil des Wohnraums.

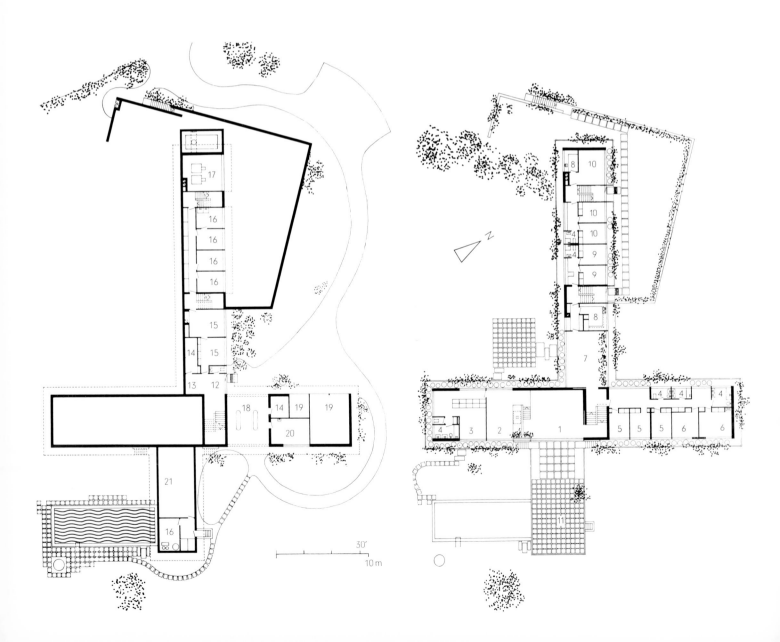

30'

10 m

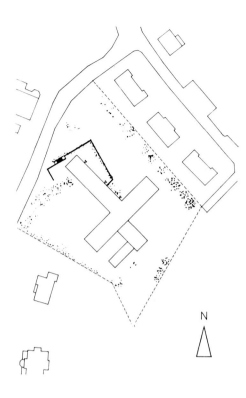

Hardenberg House at Baden-Baden, Germany
Architects: Egon Eiermann and Georg Pollich

Situated on a north slope and surrounded by older and rather unattractive houses, this partly two-storeyed house is kept deliberately unobtrusive in spite of its long front and large size. The plan is T-shaped with a longitudinal axis running from north-west to south-east and continued by the east terrace which is shifted slightly south-westwards by half the room width. The upper floor is purely residential. At the intersection of the two wings is the large living room which is exceptionally high and wide. Adjacent to it but at a higher level, which gives it a lower ceiling height, is a small lounge which is linked visually with the hall. Beyond it are master bedroom, dressing-room and bathroom. At the opposite end of the wing are the bedrooms of the three children as well as two guest rooms. These two arms of the residential wing are linked by the staircase which also connects with dining room and kitchen in the service wing. The remainder of this wing is taken up by two maid's rooms and the caretaker's flat which have separate entrances. In the lower floor are utility rooms, garage, hobby room and an office with waiting room accessible from the main entrance at lower floor level. On the north side, the utility wing is separated from the drive by a low wall. Cantilevered floor slab and projecting roof create a covered galley around the entire building. They are braced by a framework of white-painted metal tubing which also serves as a railing and as an espalier for climbing plants. The architect envisages that the plants will, in due course, form a green curtain – a kind of second skin outside the large, mostly fixed, plate-glass panels, making the rooms appear larger than they are. In time, the plants are expected to grow over the roof, thus softening the rigidity and size of the structure. Construction: load bearing walls of concrete and brick, combined with steel posts along the large window fronts. Reinforced concrete floors. 'Thermopane' windows in wooden frames. Radiant heating in ceilings and floors.

Haus Hardenberg in Baden-Baden
Architekten: Egon Eiermann und Georg Pollich

Das bei aller Weite und Größe sehr zurückhaltende, teilweise zweigeschossige Haus liegt auf einem Nordhang, umgeben von älteren, wenig ansehnlichen Häusern. Der Grundriß hat die Form eines T, dessen Längsachse von Nordwesten nach Südosten verläuft. Sie wird fortgeführt durch die nach Osten vorspringende Terrasse, die um die halbe Breite eines Hausflügels versetzt wurde. Das Obergeschoß ist als reines Wohngeschoß ausgebildet. Im Schnittpunkt der beiden Trakte liegt der große Wohnraum, der sich durch besondere Höhe und Weite auszeichnet. Im Niveau angehoben und dadurch niedriger schließt sich der kleine Wohnraum an, der optisch mit der Halle in Verbindung steht. Dahinter liegen Eltern-schlafraum mit Ankleide und Bad. Im gegenüberliegenden Teil des Flügels sind die Räume für die drei Kinder und zwei Gästezimmer zusammengefaßt. Zwischen diese beiden Arme des Wohnflügels schiebt sich als Bindeglied das Treppenhaus, das zugleich Speisezimmer und Küche mit Anrichte im Wirtschaftsflügel erschließt. Zwei Mädchenzimmer und die Hausmeisterwohnung mit eigenem Zugang beanspruchen den verbleibenden Teil dieses Flügels. Im Untergeschoß befinden sich Wirtschaftsräume, Garage, Hobbyraum und ein Büro mit Vorzimmer, zugänglich über den Haupteingang im Untergeschoß. Der Wirtschafts-trakt ist nach Norden gegen die Zufahrt durch eine niedrige Mauer abgegrenzt. Auskragende Geschoßdecke und vorspringendes Dach schaffen einen gedeckten Umgang um das ganze Gebäude. Sie sind verspannt durch ein weiß gestrichenes Metallgestänge, das gleichzeitig als Geländer und Spalier für Grünpflanzen dient. Nach der Vorstellung des Architekten soll sich so im Verlauf der Jahre vor den großen, meist fest verglasten Fensterflächen ein grüner Vorhang, eine Art zweiter Haut bilden, die die Räume größer wirken läßt. Allmählich sollen die Pflanzen auch über das Dach wachsen und damit die Härte und Größe der Bauform auflösen. Konstruktion: Tragende Wände aus Beton und Backsteinmauerwerk, kombiniert mit Stahlstützen in den großen Fensterfassaden. Stahlbetonrippendecken. Thermopane-fenster in Holzrahmen. Deckenstrahlungs- und Fußbodenheizung.

1. East side. In the centre the large living room; in front of it the terrace and, on the left, the swimming pool. On the right, the wing with the children's and guest rooms. In the lower floor, a car port open on two sides, in the recessed part are a workshop and garages.
2. Plan of lower floor (left) and upper floor. Key: 1 large living room, 2 lounge, 3 master bedroom with dressing room, 4 bathroom and W.C., 5 children's bedroom, 6 guest room, 7 dining room, 8 kitchen, 9 maid's room, 10 caretaker's flat, 11 terrace, 12 main entrance, 13 cloak room, 14 storage room, 15 office, 16 basement store, 17 boiler room, 18 car port, 19 garage, 20 and 21 hobby rooms.
3. Site plan.

1. Gesamtansicht von Osten. In der Mitte der große Wohnraum mit anschließender Terrasse und Schwimmbecken (links). Rechts Kinder- und Gästeflügel. Im Untergeschoß ein nach zwei Seiten offener Wageneinstellplatz. Im zurückgesetzten Sockel Werkstatt und Garagen.
2. Grundrisse von Untergeschoß (links) und Ober-geschoß. Legende: 1 Großer Wohnraum, 2 Klei-ner Wohnraum, 3 Elternschlafraum mit Ankleide, 4 Bad und WC, 5 Kinderzimmer, 6 Gastzimmer, 7 Speisezimmer 8 Küche, 9 Mädchenzimmer, 10 Hausmeisterwohnung, 11 Terrasse, 12 Haupt-eingang, 13 Garderobe, 14 Abstellraum, 15 Büro, 16 Kellerräume, 17 Heizraum, 18 Wageneinstell-platz, 19 Garage, 20 Bastelraum, 21 Hobbyraum.
3. Lageplan.

4. View of the service wing, with the wall surrounding the patio. Below the awning is the entrance door to caretaker's flat and maid's rooms.

5. Outdoor sitting area outside living room and dining room. In the foreground the windows of the master bedroom.

6. Outside the windows of the lounge is the swimming pool.

7. Around the upper floor runs a covered gallery, paved with gravel and circular ceramic flags which serve as stepping stones. The climbing plants on the metal tubing are expected to form a green corridor behind which the house will eventually disappear.

4. Blick auf den Wirtschaftsflügel und die den Wirtschaftshof umgrenzende Mauer. Unter dem Sonnensegel die Eingänge zur Hausmeisterwohnung und zu den Mädchenzimmern.

5. Freisitzplatz vor Wohnraum und Speisezimmer. Im Vordergrund die Fenster des Elternschlafraums.

6. Vor den Fenstern des kleinen Wohnraums liegt das Schwimmbecken.

7. Rings um das Obergeschoß läuft ein bekiester Umgang, belegt mit runden Tonplatten als Trittsteinen. Die an dem leichten Fassadengestänge hochrankenden Pflanzen sollen einen grünen Laubengang bilden, der die Innenräume optisch erweitert und hinter dem in späteren Jahren das Haus ganz verschwinden wird.

8, 9. Sliding doors lead from the large living room out to the terrace. The floor is of dark-blue glazed ceramic tiles. A short flight of stairs leads to the small high-level lounge which is separated from the main living room by the balustrade and by the open fireplace with its suspended hood. These photographs were taken before the house was furnished.

10. Part of the central staircase which connects the different wings and levels of the house. The steps are of artificial stone, the flooring of circular, partly glazed and partly unglazed ceramic tiles in different colours and sizes; the walls are of red-brown, fair-faced brick.

11. Dining room. In front of the window is a sunken flower bed whose climbers will, in due course, form a green curtain. The wooden trellis-work serves to provide greater privacy.

12. Southward view across the outdoor sitting area.

8, 9. Die große Wohnhalle öffnet sich durch Schiebetüren auf die Terrasse. Der Boden ist mit dunkelblau glasierten Tonplatten belegt. Über eine kurze Treppe gelangt man in den höher-liegenden kleinen Wohnraum. Brüstung und offener Kamin, dessen Rauchschürze frei von der Decke hängt, bilden die Begrenzung zum großen Wohnraum. Die Aufnahmen zeigen die Räume ohne Möblierung.

10. Blick in das zentrale Treppenhaus, das die verschiedenen Flügel und Ebenen des Hauses verbindet. Treppenstufen aus Kunststein; Böden aus runden glasierten und unglasierten Ton-platten in verschiedenen Farben und Größen; Wände rotbraune Vormauerungssteine.

11. Das Speisezimmer. Vor dem Fenster ein in den Boden eingelassenes Pflanzenbecken, des-sen Gewächse später einen Grünvorhang bilden werden. Holzgitterwerk als Sichtblende.

12. Blick nach Süden auf den Freisitzplatz.

1. View from west, with the courtyard formed by the three wings. As the living room wing is made transparent by full-size windows on either side, the Sound is visible from the courtyard.
2. Living room wing and parents' wing, seen from the south-east. The outdoor stairs lead to the library on the upper level of the two-storey part of the living room wing.
3. Site plan.

1. Blick von Westen in den Hof der dreiflügeligen Anlage. Da der Wohntrakt auf beiden Längsseiten verglast ist, hat man schon vom Hof aus einen Durchblick auf den Sund.
2. Wohntrakt und Elternflügel von Nordosten. Die Außentreppe führt zur Bibliothek im zweigeschossigen Teil des Wohnflügels.
3. Lageplan.

House for R. Jürgensen at Vedbaek, Denmark
Architect: Arne Jacobsen

The large site on the coast of the Sound slopes down gently towards south and east. The design of the house was to provide a good view to the east, yet allow the sun to penetrate from the south. Another complication arose from the owners' requirement that their bedrooms should be separated from those of the three children, guests and staff. The wing containing the parents' room is turned slightly south-east to obtain a view across the Sound and linked with the south facing wing for children, guests and staff by a central block containing living room, dining room and kitchen. Under the slope of its long single-pitch roof, the central block is two storeys high at the southern end with a library, and loggia on the upper level, and a conservatory and fireside lounge on the lower one. The ceiling height decreases steadily from the living room through the adjacent dining room to the kitchen. All the rooms in this wing face both east and west. Apart from the kitchen the main entrance and hall are set in the angle between this wing and the children's wing. In addition each of the bedroom wings has a separate entrance of its own. In both these wings, access to the rooms is provided through a cupboard-lined corridor, top-lit by glass domes. The architect was responsible not only for the design of the house but also for most of the furniture and for the garden. Construction: Central block: steel frame structure with wooden boarding outside and inside and with 'Thermopane' windows. Bedroom wings: brick construction with large wood framed windows. With the exception of the teak floor in the library, all floors are of plastic tiles. Floor heating, supplemented by radiators in the bedrooms.

Haus R. Jürgensen in Vedbaek, Dänemark
Architekt: Arne Jacobsen

Das große Grundstück am Öresund fällt leicht nach Süden und Osten ab. Bei der Grundrißdisposition war einerseits die Aussicht nach Osten auf den Sund zu berücksichtigen und trotzdem die Südsonne in die Räume hereinzuholen. Dazu kam noch der ausdrückliche Wunsch des Bauherrn, die Zimmer für seine drei Kinder, Gäste und Personal getrennt von den Schlafräumen der Eltern in einem besonderen Trakt zusammenzufassen. Der leicht nach Südosten abgedrehte Elternflügel mit Blick auf den Sund und der genau nach Süden orientierte Kindertrakt werden durch einen dritten Flügel verbunden, in dem Wohnraum, Eßzimmer und Küche untergebracht sind. Durch das Ansteigen des Pultdaches war es möglich, den Wohntrakt am Südende zweigeschossig auszubilden: unter der Bibliothek und der Loggia im Obergeschoß liegen im Erdgeschoß Wintergarten und Kaminzimmer. Vom Wohnraum nimmt die Raumhöhe über das anschließende Eßzimmer bis zur Küche kontinuierlich ab. Alle Räume des Wohnflügels werden von Osten und Westen belichtet. Haupteingang und Diele liegen im Winkel zwischen Wohn- und Kindertrakt. Eltern- und Kinderflügel haben darüber hinaus noch separate Nebeneingänge. Beide Schlaftrakte sind über einen Schrankflur mit Oberlichtkuppeln zugänglich. Die Einrichtung ist im wesentlichen vom Architekten entworfen, nach dessen Plänen auch die Gartenanlagen ausgeführt wurden. Konstruktion: Wohnflügel Stahlrahmenkonstruktion, innen und außen mit Holzriemen verkleidet, Thermopanefenster. Nebentrakte Backsteinbauten mit großen Holzfenstern. Fußböden Kunststoff-Fliesen, nur in der Bibliothek Teakfußboden. Fußbodenheizung, in den Schlafräumen zusätzlich Radiatoren.

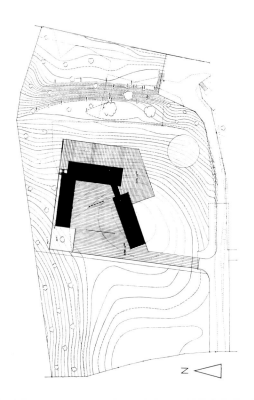

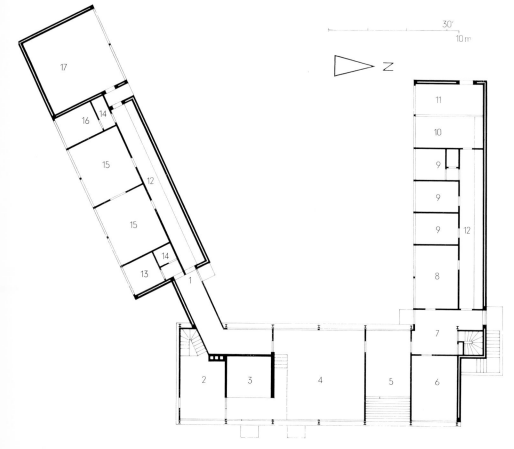

4. Living room, with the indoor stairs leading to the library.
5. Dining room and living room are separated by a screen partition with fixed glazing above. The incline of the roof is visible right up to the library window on the upper level.
6. Plan. Key: 1 entrance and hall, 2 conservatory, 3 fireside lounge, 4 living room, 5 dining room, 6 kitchen, 7 pantry, 8 guest room, 9 children's room, 10 maid's room, 11 storage room, 12 cupboard corridor, 13 cloakroom, 14 W.C., 15 parent's bedrooms, 16 bathroom, 17 garage.

4. Blick in den Wohnraum mit der Treppe zur Bibliothek.
5. Eßplatz und Wohnraum sind durch eine Schirmwand voneinander getrennt, die in ihrem oberen Teil fest verglast ist. Der Blick kann ungehindert der Dachschräge folgen bis hinauf zum Fenster der Bibliothek im Obergeschoß.
6. Grundriß. Legende: 1 Eingang und Diele, 2 Wintergarten, 3 Kaminzimmer, 4 Wohnraum, 5 Eßzimmer, 6 Küche, 7 Anrichte und Speisekammer, 8 Gastzimmer, 9 Kinderzimmer, 10 Mädchenzimmer, 11 Abstellraum, 12 Schrankflur, 13 Garderobe, 14 WC, 15 Elternschlafraum, 16 Bad, 17 Garage.

7. Living room and adjacent dining room are seen from the high-level library. The windows facing the courtyard are designed as glass display cabinets.

8. Passage between living room and conservatory; above the passage are the stairs leading to the library.

9. View from the living room terrace towards the Sound. The stone slabs are laid with ½ in. joints in which hardy moss is planted.

10. The conservatory faces south and east. Suspended above the glass-encased flower bed, which was designed by the architect himself, are orchids – their tangled roots exposed. On the terrace outside are the outdoor stairs leading to the upper level library.

7. Blick von der Bibliothek in den Wohnraum mit dem anschließenden Eßzimmer. Die Fenster zum Hof sind als Vitrinen ausgebildet.

8. Durchgang vom Wohnraum zum Wintergarten. Darüber die Treppe zur Bibliothek.

9. Blick von der Terrasse vor dem Wohnraum auf den Sund. Die Steinplatten wurden mit einem Zwischenraum von einem Zentimeter verlegt und in die Fugen widerstandsfähiges Moos gepflanzt.

10. Der Wintergarten öffnet sich nach Süden und Osten. Im Vordergrund das allseitig verglaste, vom Architekten angelegte Pflanzenbecken, darüber die mit ihren Wurzelballen aufgehängten Orchideen. Auf der Terrasse ist die zur Bibliothek führende Außentreppe zu erkennen.

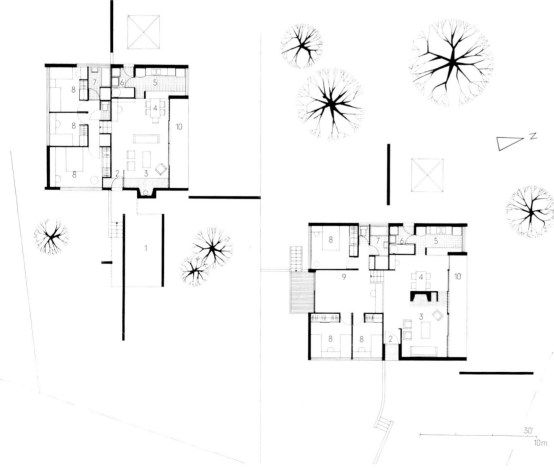

Two houses at Carlingford, New South Wales, Australia
Architect: Harry Seidler and Associates

These houses, standing on a south slope, demonstrate how adjacent houses can be designed to complement each other and to create privacy and sympathetic space relationships between them. The aim was to produce economically planned and constructed houses which could be adapted to the varying site conditions. Although the plans are basically similar they permit considerable flexibility inside as well as outside. Both houses adjust to the slope with split-levels; their living rooms face the sunny side, i. e. north. The bedrooms are on the south side. Kitchen, utility room and bathroom are all on the west side. The somewhat larger house, located uphill, has two storeys on the south side. The lower floor serves as a garage for two cars; on the upper floor, the bedrooms of the parents and two children are grouped around the central play area which is connected directly with the garden via a balcony and an outside stairway. Inside the house, a few steps lead down to the living room which is half a storey lower. The living room, entered through a small lobby from the main entrance, gives access to all the other rooms. Construction: facing bricks and concrete blocks; outer walls partly painted white, blue or mustard colour.

Zwei Häuser in Carlingford, Neusüdwales, Australien
Architekt: Harry Seidler & Associates

Auf einem Südhang wurde für eine Ausstellung eine Gebäudegruppe erstellt, die zeigen sollte, wie sich benachbarte Einfamilienhäuser formal aufeinander abstimmen lassen und sowohl gegeneinander abgeschlossen oder aber, soweit erwünscht, miteinander verbunden werden können. Die Entwürfe, die in Grundriß und Konstruktion sehr wirtschaftlich sind, lassen sich mit einfachen Änderungen an die verschiedensten Grundstücksverhältnisse anpassen. Bei gleich angelegtem Grundriß ist dennoch innen wie außen eine beträchtliche Variabilität erreicht. Beide Häuser passen sich mit versetzten Geschossen dem Gefälle an und sind mit ihren Wohnräumen nach Norden, zur Sonnenseite, orientiert. Die Schlafräume liegen in der Südhälfte. Küche, Hauswirtschaftsraum und Bad sind auf der Westseite zusammengefaßt. Das auf dem oberen Teil des Hanges stehende, etwas größere Haus ist in seinem Südteil zweigeschossig. Das Untergeschoß dient als Garage für zwei Wagen; im Obergeschoß sind das Eltern- und zwei Kinderschlafzimmer um ein zentrales Spielzimmer gruppiert, das über Balkon und Außentreppe direkt mit dem Garten verbunden ist. Im Hausinnern führen einige Stufen zu dem um ein halbes Geschoß versetzten Wohnraum hinunter. Vom Wohnraum aus, den man über einen kleinen Vorplatz hinter der Haustür betritt, werden alle übrigen Räume erschlossen. Konstruktion: Sichtmauerwerk aus Ziegeln und Zementsteinen. Dach Holzkonstruktion. Außenwände zum Teil weiß, blau oder senffarben gestrichen.

1. The two houses seen from the road on the east side. The slope of the single-pitch roof of the lower house follows the slope of the ground whilst that of the house on the right is set against the slope.
2. Plan. Key: 1 car port, 2 entrance, 3 living area with fireplace, 4 dining area, 5 kitchen, 6 utility room, 7 bathroom, 8 bedroom, 9 play area, 10 terrace.
3. The smaller, lower house seen from the east. The carefully related textures and colours of the various masses and surfaces produce an attractive overall picture. The open car port in front of the house is self-contained. Its overhanging roof forms a covered access.

1. Ansicht der beiden Häuser von Osten, von der Straße aus. Bei dem tieferliegenden Haus links folgt das Pultdach der Hanglinie, während bei dem Haus rechts die Dachneigung der Hangneigung entgegengesetzt ist.
2. Grundriß. Legende: 1 Wageneinstellhalle, 2 Eingang, 3 Wohnbereich mit Kamin, 4 Eßplatz, 5 Küche, 6 Hauswirtschaftsraum, 7 Bad, 8 Schlafraum, 9 Kinderspielraum, 10 Terrasse.
3. Ansicht des tieferliegenden, kleineren Hauses von Osten. Kuben und Flächen mit sorgfältig aufeinander abgestimmten Texturen und Farben ergeben ein differenziertes Gesamtbild. Die offene Wageneinstellhalle ist frei vor das Haus gesetzt. Ihr auskragendes Dach bildet einen überdeckten Zugang.

4. North side of the smaller house with living room terrace. On the right, the high-level window of the kitchen.

5. Free-standing screen walls create privacy and wind protection for open courtyards.

6. Lower house, seen from the balcony of the upper house. On the left the self-contained car port. On the east side of the living area, the fireplace and its cylindrical chimney are visible.

7. The living room of the upper house, with the entrance at the far right, seen from the play area which is on the higher lever.

4. Die Nordseite des kleineren Hauses mit der Terrasse vor dem Wohnraum. Rechts das hochliegende Fenster der Küche.

5. Frei stehende Schirmwände schaffen wind- und sichtgeschützte Sitzplätze im Freien.

6. Blick vom Balkon des höherliegenden Hauses auf das Nachbargebäude. Links die frei stehende Wageneinstellhalle. An der Ostseite des Wohnteils ist außen die Ummantelung des Kamins und der zylindrische Schornstein zu erkennen.

7. Blick vom höherliegenden Spielzimmer in den Wohnraum des oberen Hauses. Ganz rechts der Eingang.

8. Section of both houses.
9. The free-standing fireplace divides the north main room into a living and a dining area. The roof projecting over the recessed window wall provides ample sun protection.

8. Schnitt durch beide Häuser.
9. Der frei stehende Kamin teilt den Hauptraum des nördlichen Hausteils in einen Wohn- und einen Eßbereich. Das auskragende Dach über der zurückgesetzten Fensterfront gibt bei hohem Sonnenstand ausreichenden Sonnenschutz.

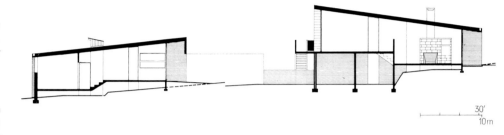

30'
10m

1. East side. The building appears to be floating, an impression which is contributed to by the slender open steel columns of the lower floor. The entrance proper is on the left, via the stairs along the retaining wall.
2. Site plan.

1. Blick von Osten. Der Baukörper scheint zu schweben, ein Eindruck, der durch die schlanken, durchbrochenen Stahlstützen des Untergeschosses verstärkt wird. Der offizielle Zugang erfolgt links über die Treppe vor der Stützmauer.
2. Lageplan.

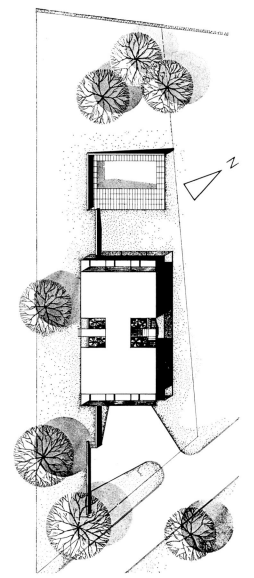

House for P. Drill at West Orange, New Jersey
Architects: Lewis Davis, Samuel Brody and Associates

The deep and narrow site is divided by a bank down its length into a high level area with many trees and a low level area forming an open meadow. One long side of the house stands on the upper level supported by a long brick retaining wall. The main floor, raised slightly above the higher ground level, is divided into two distinct areas, one for living and one for sleeping. These two areas are linked by the hall which is set like a bridge between two open wells recessed into the building. The house is entered through the patio on the higher side whilst the patio on the opposite side contains the spiral staircase leading to the lower floor which houses the car port. As the east side affords a dramatic view of the New York skyline, the living area was placed on this side. By placing the kitchen as an island in the centre, the living area has been divided into separate areas, two for sitting, one for dining, and one for breakfast. In the bedroom area, the design approach is similar: the bedrooms for the family of four are grouped around a central core, composed of bathroom, shower bath and W.C. A children's playroom is inserted between the two children's bedrooms on the south side and the master bedroom in the north-west corner. As there are other houses close to the north and south sides, the long sides are closed but for narrow vertical strip windows at the corners, and the privacy of the patios and balconies is protected by wooden grilles. Similar horizontal grilles, made of redwood, are provided for the balconies on the east and west sides. These grilles, which are top-hung and pivoted from the roof beams, can be swung out at various angles, up to 90°. The lower level is open, and includes a car port andcovered terrace. Behind the retaining wall are the boiler and storage rooms. Construction: Steel frame with cruciform columns comprising four steel angles (2″ × 2″ × ½″) and 2″ wide steel plates serving as spacers. The structural deck is supported by beams set on edge, consisting of two steel plates with spacers. Ceilings and floors are prefabricated wooden parts. Floor heating.

Haus P. Drill in West Orange, New Jersey
Architekten: Lewis Davis, Samuel Brody & Associates

Das schmale und tiefe Grundstück ist der Länge nach durch eine Geländestufe in einen oberen, mit Bäumen bestandenen und einen unteren, mit Gras bewachsenen Bereich unterteilt. Das Haus ruht mit einer Längsseite auf der höheren, durch eine lange Backsteinmauer abgestützten Stufe und ragt mit drei Vierteln seiner Breite darüber hinaus. Das Wohngeschoß, das etwas über das Niveau der oberen Geländestufe angehoben wurde, gliedert sich in zwei deutlich voneinander abgesetzte Zonen: den Schlaf- und den Wohnteil. Diese beiden Zonen sind durch die Diele verbunden, die wie eine Brücke zwischen zwei atriumartig aus dem Baukörper ausgesparten Höfen liegt. Man betritt das Haus über den Hof auf der Bergseite, während der gegenüberliegende Hof die Wendeltreppe zum Untergeschoß mit dem Wageneinstellplatz aufnimmt. Da man nach Osten einen großartigen Blick auf die Skyline von New York hat, wurde der Wohnteil auf diese Seite gelegt. Die inselartig in den Raum gesetzte Küche schafft verschiedene Bereiche: Sitzgruppe, Eßplatz und eine zweite Sitzgruppe mit dahinterliegendem Frühstücksplatz. Im Schlafbereich ist die Situation ähnlich: um einen Kern mit Bad, Dusche und Toilette gruppieren sich die Schlafräume der vierköpfigen Familie. Zwischen die beiden Kinderzimmer auf der Südseite und das Elternschlafzimmer in der Nordwestecke ist ein Spielzimmer eingeschoben. Da nach Norden und Süden Nachbarbauten angrenzen, sind die Längsfronten bis auf schmale, senkrechte Fensterstreifen an den Ecken geschlossen und die Höfe sowie die Balkonseiten durch Blenden aus Holzlatten gegen Einblick geschützt. Das Motiv der horizontalen Sichtblenden wurde von den Balkons auf der Ost- und Westseite übernommen, deren Brüstungen aus den gleichen Redwoodleisten bestehen. Holzscreens, die am Stirnbalken der Dachkonstruktion drehbar befestigt sind, können in verschiedenen Stellungen arretiert oder um volle 90 Grad nach außen geschwenkt werden. Das freibleibende Untergeschoß wird als Wageneinstellplatz und überdachte Terrasse genutzt. Hinter der Stützmauer liegen Heiz- und Abstellraum. Konstruktion: Stahlrahmen mit kreuzförmigen Stützen, die aus 4 Winkeleisen (2″ × 2″ × ½″) und 2″ breiten Stahlbändern als Abstandhalter zusammengesetzt sind. Die Geschoßplatte wird von hochkant stehenden Balken aus doppelten Stahlplatten mit Abstandhaltern getragen. Decke und Boden aus vorfabrizierten Holzelementen. Fußboden-Warmluftheizung.

3. West side, with the balcony grilles closed. All the large windows of the house are given privacy and sun protection by these grilles which are partly fixed and partly adjustable. The retaining wall, which forms a right angle in the foreground, defines the outdoor sitting and playing area below the house.

4. From the lower floor, a spiral flight of stairs with wooden treads in the north patio leads to the upper floor hall.

3. Westansicht mit geschlossenen Lamellenblenden vor dem Balkon. Alle großen Fensterflächen des Hauses sind durch diese teils fest eingebauten, teils beweglichen Screens gegen Einsicht und Sonne geschützt. Die rechtwinklig abgeknickte Stützmauer grenzt den Sitz- und Spielbereich unter dem Haus ein.

4. Vom Untergeschoß aus führt eine Wendeltreppe mit Holzstufen durch den atriumartigen Nordhof zur Diele im Wohngeschoß.

5, 6. The difference in level caused by raising the house above the upper ground level is overcome by four steps. A wooden bridge leads across the recessed south patio to the main entrance and hall. In the background is the door of the north patio. The wells on the left and right of the access bridge are designed to take flower tubs. The adjacent rooms face the entrance patio with storey-high windows and glass sliding doors.
7. Plans of main floor (top) and lower floor. Key: 1 entrance and hall, 2 sitting area, 3 dining area, 4 kitchen, 5 master bedroom with study, 6 bathroom and W.C., 7 children's playroom, 8 children's bedroom, 9 covered terrace, 10 boiler room, 11 carpet, 12 storage room.

5, 6. Vier Stufen überwinden den Niveauunterschied, der sich aus der Anhebung des Baukörpers über die obere Geländeebene ergibt. Eine Holzbrücke führt quer über den eingezogenen Südhof hinweg zu Hauseingang und Diele. Im Hintergrund die Tür zum Nordhof. Die Schächte links und rechts vom Zugangssteg nehmen Pflanzenkübel auf. Die anschließenden Räume öffnen sich mit raumhohen Fenstern und Glasschiebetüren auf den Eingangshof.
7. Grundrisse von Wohngeschoß (oben) und Untergeschoß. Legende: 1 Eingang und Diele, 2 Sitzgruppen im Wohnraum, 3 Eßplatz, 4 Küche, 5 Elternschlafraum mit Studio, 6 Bad und WC, 7 Spielzimmer, 8 Kinderzimmer, 9 Gedeckte Terrasse, 10 Heizraum, 11 Wageneinstellplatz, 12 Abstellraum.

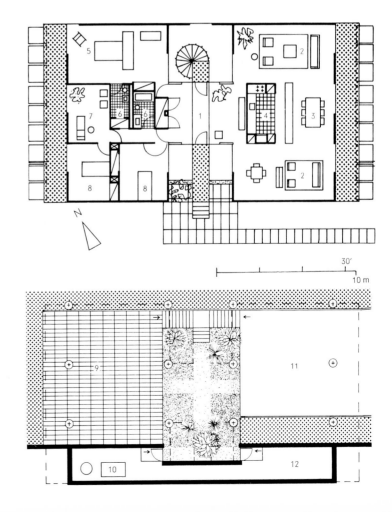

8. Living room balcony with the grilles tilted up.
9, 10. Kitchen 'island' and dining area in the living room. If desired, the kitchen can be hidden behind folding doors giving the appearance of a large cupboard unit. Bar, cupboard walls and doors are of the same kind of wood. The kitchen has toplighting flush with the wooden ceiling between the dark-painted roof beams which are left visible, and direct roof ventilation.

8. Blick auf den Balkon vor dem Wohnteil mit hochgeklappten Blenden.
9, 10. Küchen-»Insel« und Eßplatz im Wohnteil. Bei Bedarf verschwindet die Küche hinter Falttüren und erscheint dann als großes Schrankelement. Für Theke, Schrankwände und Türen ist das gleiche Holz verwendet. Ein Oberlicht in der Holzlamellendecke zwischen den sichtbar belassenen, dunkel gestrichenen Deckenbalken belichtet die Küche, die direkt durch das Dach entlüftet wird.

11. On its long side the house is made transparent by the large patio windows. The view, from one of the sitting areas in the living room, is through the north patio with the spiral staircase towards the study which is part of the master bedroom.
12. Study and master bedroom are separated by a cupboard wall which, like the kitchen cupboard units, stops just short of the ceiling.
13. One of the bathrooms which receives daylight through a skylight in the ceiling.

11. Große Glasflächen um die Innenhöfe machen das Haus in der Längsrichtung transparent. Blick von einer der Sitzgruppen des Wohnteils über den Nordhof mit der Wendeltreppe auf das Studio.
12. Studio und Elternschlafraum sind durch einen raumteilenden Schrank getrennt, der ebenso wie die Schrankelemente der Küche nicht ganz bis zur Decke reicht.
13. Blick in ein Badezimmer, das durch eine Öffnung in der Decke Tageslicht erhält.

1. South-west side. The upper floor and living room balcony between the trees whose crowns act, during the summer, as sun and heat filters. The space outside the ground floor playroom provides the children with an ideal playground. The bedroom wing is on the left.

1. Ansicht des Südwestflügels. Das Obergeschoß mit Balkon und Wohnraum stößt zwischen die Stämme vor, deren Kronen im Sommer als Licht- und Hitzefilter wirken. Vor dem ebenerdigen Spielzimmer finden die Kinder ein ideales Spiel- gelände. Links der Schlafflügel.

House for W. Shuttleworth at Cedar Rapids, Iowa
Architects: Ray D. Crites and R. D. McConnell

The wooded site on which this two-storey timber house has been erected slopes steeply down on three sides. The cruciform plan allowed for an easy integration of the building with its forest setting. The trees cluster closely around the living room and master bedroom on all three sides. The entrance is at the point where the wings intersect. The lower floor, reserved for the three children, contains a large playroom, two bedrooms with bath, and a utility room. In response to the owner's wishes, the upper floor rooms have been so arranged that his study in the north-east wing is as far away as possible from the playroom. At the opposite end, facing south-west, is the living room which projects over the ground floor and contains an open fireplace. Arranged lengthwise from south-east to north-west are the open car port, kitchen, dining room, closets, bathroom and W.C. At the end is the master bedroom. No room shares more than one wall with another room so that mutual disturbance is minimized. The cruciform plan favours the provision of outdoor sitting areas protected on several sides. Construction: Timber framework with plywood box girders. Walls and ceiling faced with timber boards. External facing of cedar wood fillets set horizontally. All other timber framing is clad with plastic-faced plywood. Gas-fired warm air heating.

Haus W. Shuttleworth in Cedar Rapids, Iowa
Architekten: Ray D. Crites und R. D. McConnell

Das mit Bäumen bestandene Grundstück, auf dem das zweigeschossige Holzhaus errichtet wurde, fällt nach drei Seiten stark ab. Durch den kreuzförmigen Grundriß wurde die Einbettung des Baukörpers in den umgebenden Wald noch verstärkt: bei Wohnraum und Elternschlafzimmer rücken die Bäume auf drei Seiten dicht heran. Das Haus wird vom Zentrum im Schnittpunkt der Kreuzarme aus erschlossen. Das Untergeschoß, das den drei Kindern vorbehalten ist, umfaßt ein großes Spielzimmer, zwei Schlafräume mit Bad und einen Hauswirtschaftsraum. Die Anordnung der Räume im Obergeschoß ist auf Wunsch des Hausherrn so gewählt, daß sein Arbeitszimmer möglichst weit vom Spielzimmer entfernt im Nordost-Flügel liegt. Gegenüber befindet sich, nach Südwesten orientiert, der über das Untergeschoß auskragende Wohnraum mit offenem Kamin. In der Längsachse sind der offene Wageneinstellplatz, Küche, Eßplatz, Schrankräume, Bad und WC hintereinandergereiht. Am Ende liegt der Elternschlafraum. Kein Raum hat mehr als eine Wand mit einem anderen gemeinsam, wodurch Störquellen weitgehend ausgeschaltet werden. Die Grundrißform begünstigt die Anlage mehrseitig geschützter Freisitzplätze. Konstruktion: Holzrahmenwerk mit Sperrholz-Kastenträgern. Wände und Decken mit Holzplatten verkleidet. Am Außenbau waagrechte Schalung aus Zedernholzriemen; übrige Holzteile mit Kunstharz imprägnierte Sperrholzverkleidung. Gasbefeuerte Warmluftheizung.

2. East side. On the extreme left is the tool shed, next to it the door leading to the car port. On the right the north-east wing with the study. In the centre are the windows of the dining room, and in front of it a terrace which is shared by dining room and study.

2. Ansicht von Osten. Links der Geräteschuppen, daneben die Tür zum Wageneinstellplatz. Rechts der Nordostflügel mit dem Arbeitszimmer. In der Mitte die Fensterwand des Eßplatzes, davor eine Terrasse, die Eßplatz und Arbeitszimmer zugeordnet ist.

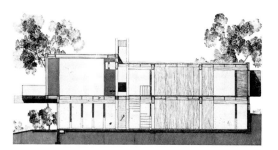

3. Seen from south-east, the house is hidden behind trees and the open car port. The sliding door on the right is that of the tool shed.
4. The approach path on south side leads past the kitchen terrace to the main entrance at the intersection of the cruciform wings.

3. Von Südosten gesehen liegt das Haus hinter Bäumen und dem Wageneinstellplatz versteckt. Rechts die Schiebetür des Geräteschuppens.
4. Der Zugang auf der Südseite führt an der Küchenterrasse vorbei zum Eingang im Schnittpunkt der beiden Kreuzarme.

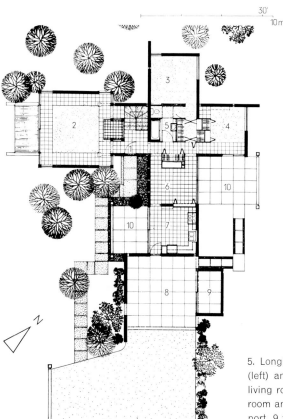

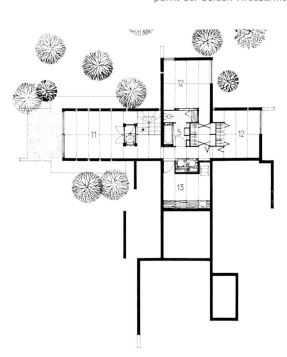

5. Longitudinal section and plans of lower floor (left) and upper floor. Key: 1 entrance hall, 2 living room, 3 master bedroom, 4 study, 5 bathroom and W.C., 6 dining room, 7 kitchen, 8 car port, 9 tool shed, 10 terrace, 11 children's playroom, 12 children's bedroom, 13 utility room.

5. Längsschnitt und Grundrisse von Unter- und Obergeschoß. Legende: 1 Eingang, 2 Wohnraum, 3 Elternschlafraum, 4 Arbeitszimmer, 5 Bad und WC, 6 Eßzimmer, 7 Küche, 8 Wageneinstellplatz, 9 Geräteschuppen, 10 Terrasse, 11 Spielzimmer, 12 Kinderzimmer, 13 Hauswirtschaftsraum.

6. South side. The window openings of the children's playroom below the projecting living room are repeated at the staircase.

7. Through the room-high windows and glazed sliding door leading to the balcony, daylight can penetrate freely.

8. Main entrance: on the left the living room and, below it, the children's playroom.

9. Behind the fireplace in the living room are the stairs leading to the lower floor. On the right is the passage to the entrance and centre of the house. For economic reasons, the dimensions and designs of the originally envisaged concrete structure had to be translated into timber. The box-shaped light fittings are designed as bulk heads and are similar to those used outside.

6. Blick von Süden. Die Lichtschlitze des Spielzimmers unter dem auskragenden Wohnraum wiederholen sich am Treppenhaus.

7. Raumhohe Fenster und die vollverglaste Schiebetür zum Balkon lassen das in allen Farben spielende Licht ungehindert in den Raum dringen.

8. Blick auf Haupteingang, Wohnraum und den darunterliegenden Aufenthaltsraum der Kinder.

9. Hinter dem Kamin des Wohnraums die Treppe zum Untergeschoß. Rechts die Passage zum Eingang und zum Hauskern. Maße und Formen der ursprünglich in Beton geplanten Konstruktion sind aus Budgetgründen in Holz übertragen. Kastenförmige Beleuchtungskörper als Balkenkopf ausgebildet, ähnlich auch am Außenbau verwendet.

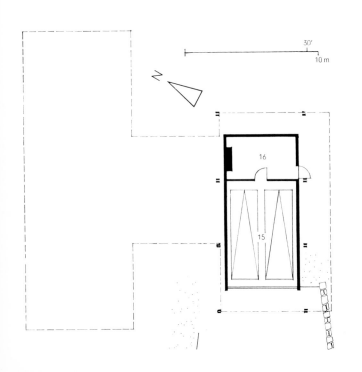

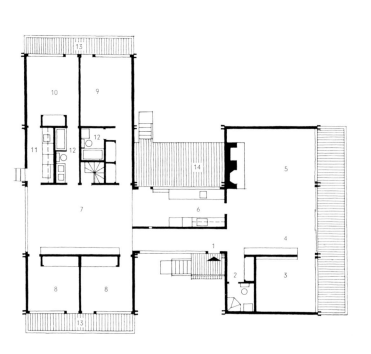

House for W. Abruzzi at Wappinger Falls, New York
Architect: Jay Fleishman

The client needed, for his family of four, a house that would provide separate adults' and children's living spaces, yet allow the wife visual control of both areas from the kitchen. Each room was required to have direct access to a balcony or terrace. In the resulting H-shaped plan the two parallel wings, containing the bedrooms and living room respectively, are linked by a narrow wing containing kitchen, hall and entrance. The site is on a heavily wooded hilltop and to avoid costly rock blasting the house was built on stilts. The space between the south wing columns is used as a garage; behind it are the boiler room and storage room. Above them on the main floor are the living room with dining area and a study, both have large south-facing windows. The rooms in the single-storey bedroom wing are grouped around a spacious hall which serves as play area for the children and as circulation area between the two children's rooms on the west side and the master bedroom and guest room on the east wide. The adults' bedrooms are screened from the hall by bathrooms and cupboard units. Construction: Timber post-and-beam structure with cedar wood cladding; basement of the two-storey part built of concrete bricks, with fascias of asbestos cement board. Timber roof.

Haus W. Abruzzi in Wappinger Falls, New York
Architekt: Jay Fleishman

Der Bauherr wünschte für seine vierköpfige Familie ein Haus mit klarer Trennung des Wohn- und Schlafteils. Die Küche war so zu legen, daß die Hausfrau von dort aus die Kinder im Spielzimmer beaufsichtigen konnte. Jeder Raum sollte eine Freifläche in Form eines Balkons oder einer Terrasse zugeordnet bekommen. Der Grundriß hat die Form eines H: zwei parallel gestellte Baukörper – Schlaf- und Wohnteil – sind durch ein schmales Zwischenglied miteinander verbunden, das Küche, Flur und Eingang aufnimmt. Um auf dem Grundstück, einer dicht bewaldeten Hügelkuppe, kostspieligen Felssprengungen aus dem Wege zu gehen, wurde das Haus auf Stützen gestellt und nicht unterkellert. Der Raum zwischen den Stützen des Südflügels ist als Garage ausgebaut, dahinter liegen Heizung und Vorratsraum. Das Wohngeschoß darüber umfaßt den Wohnraum mit Eßplatz und das Studio, beide nach Süden hin durch große Glasfenster geöffnet. Die Räume des eingeschossigen Schlaftraktes gruppieren sich um eine geräumige Spieldiele, die als Verkehrsfläche die beiden Kinderzimmer auf der Westseite und den Elternschlafraum sowie das Gästezimmer – beide nach Osten orientiert – erschließt. Zur Spieldiele hin sind Badezimmer und Einbauschränke dazwischengeschaltet, die den Schlafbereich der Erwachsenen abschirmen. Holzskelettkonstruktion mit Zedernholz verschalt, Untergeschoß aus Zementblocksteinen gemauert und mit Asbestzementplatten verkleidet. Dach Holzkonstruktion.

1. West side with access road and garage below the living room wing. The entrance is placed on the linking wing. On the left the bedroom wing with the two children's rooms. The owner is a collector of south-east Asian and Polynesian art and the concave roof shells are a little reminiscent of pagoda roofs.
2. Plans of lower floor (left) and main floor. Key: 1 entrance and connecting passage, 2 cloakroom, 3 study, 4 dining area, 5 living room, 6 kitchen with breakfast area, 7 hall serving as children's playroom, 8 children's bedroom, 9 master bedroom, 10 guest room, 11 utility room, 12 bathroom, 13 balcony, 14 kitchen terrace, 15 garage, 16 boiler and storage room.
3. Rear of the house. The master bedroom and guest room are in the bedroom wing (right).

1. Westansicht mit Zufahrt und Garage unter dem Wohnflügel. Der Eingang liegt in der Querspange. Links im Schlaftrakt die beiden Kinderzimmer. Die konkav geschwungenen Dachschalen lassen an Pagodendächer denken. Der Hausherr sammelt südostasiatische und polynesische Kunst.
2. Grundrisse von Untergeschoß (links) und Erdgeschoß. Legende: 1 Eingang und Verbindungsflur, 2 Garderobe, 3 Studio, 4 Eßplatz, 5 Wohnraum, 6 Küche mit Frühstücksplatz, 7 Spieldiele, 8 Kinderzimmer, 9 Elternschlafraum, 10 Gastzimmer, 11 Hausarbeitsraum, 12 Bad, 13 Balkon, 14 Küchenterrasse, 15 Garage, 16 Heizung und Vorratsraum.
3. Die Rückseite des Hauses. Im Schlafflügel (rechts) Elternschlafraum und Gästezimmer.

4. South side of living room wing.
5. Access is through the patio between the two main wings of the house.
6. The passage connecting the living room wing with the bedroom wing has small niches to accommodate the owner's art collection. In the background is the hall which serves as playroom.
7. View from the playroom hall along the narrow connecting passage. On the left, the kitchen with breakfast area; on the right, the entrance passage; in the background the dining area in the living room is seen.

4. Südfront des Wohnraumflügels.
5. Der Zugang führt durch den Hof zwischen den beiden Haustrakten.

6. Die Passage zwischen Wohn- und Schlafflügel ist mit schmalen Wandnischen als Galerie für die Sammlung des Hausherrn gestaltet. Im Hintergrund die Spieldiele.
7. Blick von der Spieldiele in den schmalen Verbindungstrakt. Links Küche mit Frühstücksplatz, rechts Galerie und Eingang. Im Hintergrund der Eßplatz im Wohnraum.

8, 9. Two views of the living room. The concave roof is supported by laminated wood beams which taper slightly at their ends. The bands of clerestory windows give the ceiling an appearance of floating.

8, 9. Zwei Ansichten des Wohnraums. Das konkave Dach ruht auf Schichtholzbindern, die sich zu den Balkenköpfen hin verjüngen. Oberlichtbänder lassen die Decke abgehoben erscheinen.

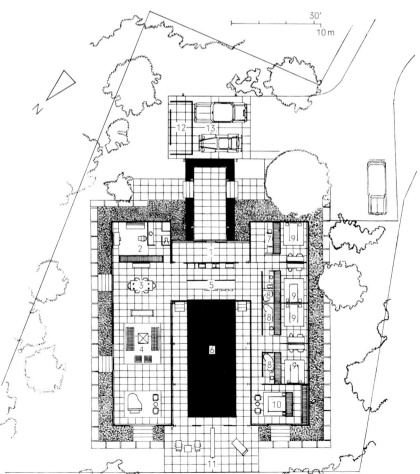

1. North side of the house, seen from the golf course. From the corner rooms of the two wings, steps lead down to the level of the terrace onto which the patio opens. Beyond the swimming pool the cross wing with kitchen and breakfast bar is visible.

2. Plan. Key: 1 entrance and hall, 2 study, 3 dining area, 4 living room, 5 kitchen with breakfast bar, 6 swimming pool, 7 utility room, 8 bathroom and W.C., 9 children's bedroom, 10 master bedroom, 11 terrace, 12 storage room, 13 car port.

3. Entrance with bridge deck connecting the car port with the entrance hall.

1. Die Nordseite des Hauses vom Golfplatz aus gesehen. Von den beiden Eckräumen der Flügel führen Stufen hinunter auf das Niveau der Terrasse, auf die sich das Atrium öffnet. Über das Schwimmbecken hinweg blickt man auf die Querspange mit Küche und Frühstücksplatz.

2. Grundriß. Legende: 1 Eingang und Diele, 2 Studio, 3 Eßplatz, 4 Wohnraum, 5 Küche mit Frühstücksplatz, 6 Schwimmbecken, 7 Hauswirtschaftsraum, 8 Bad und WC, 9 Kinderzimmer, 10 Elternschlafraum, 11 Terrasse, 12 Abstellraum, 13 Wageneinstellplatz.

3. Blick auf den Eingang mit dem Brückendeck zwischen Wageneinstellplatz und Diele.

Daphne House at Hillsborough, California
Architect: Craig Ellwood

Although the site is small for a house of this size, the architect was able to create an impression of spaciousness as the house is screened from its neighbours by trees and shrubs and is bordered on the north side by a golf course. The house is set close to the northern boundary of the site which merges with the course without visible separation, with the result that the golf course appears to belong to the house. The square plan is based on a module of 71 × 71 cm (28 × 28 in.), which is evident in the white terrazzo floor tiles, in the width of the wall panels, and in the window partitions. The two main wings linked by a cross wing form a U-shaped setting for the swimming pool which, because of the importance attached to it by the whole family, forms the centre of the house. In the west wing are five bedrooms, three with bathrooms along their inside wall. Almost the entire east wing is taken up by the living room which is subdivided into dining and sitting areas, separated from each other by the island fireplace, and a 'music room' with a grand piano. At the south end of this wing is a small study. In the linking wing is the kitchen with breakfast bar which is closed off on the entrance side by a wall unit, and serves as a passage between living room and bedroom wing. At the entrance, the south front of the house is set back creating a recess accessible from a covered bridge deck. This deck, supported by columns standing in a pool of water, is entered via a few steps from the side. The disciplined, strictly logical arrangement of the plan is matched by the precision of the structural design. Slender steel columns carry the structural deck which is raised four steps above the ground. A surround of dark pebbles bordered by a flag-paved paths give the illusion of continuing beneath the house. This feature, together with the recessing of the walls behind the columns, makes the house appear to float. Transparency is achieved by the use of storey-high coloured glass panes, broken only by an occasional wall panels of Pentelic marble, so that the apparent weightlessness of the bearing structure is emphasised. The structural floor is of concrete, the flat roof of timber.

Haus Daphne in Hillsborough, California
Architekt: Craig Ellwood

Obwohl der Bauplatz für ein Haus dieser Größe relativ knapp bemessen war, konnte der Architekt eine weiträumige und großzügige Lösung schaffen, weil Bäume und Büsche gegen die Nachbarhäuser abschirmen und sich nach Norden ein Golfplatz anschließt. Der Baukörper ist dicht an die Nordgrenze des Grundstücks gerückt, das ohne sichtbare Markierung in das Wiesengelände übergeht: der Golfplatz erscheint so optisch als zum Haus gehörig. Dem quadratischen Grundriß liegt ein Modul von 71 × 71 cm zugrunde, der auch in den weißen Terrazzoplatten des Fußbodens, in der Breite der Wandpanels und in der Fensterteilung sichtbar wird. Zwei Flügel, die durch einen Quertrakt verbunden sind, legen sich U-förmig um das Schwimmbecken. Entsprechend der Bedeutung, die ihm von der sechsköpfigen Familie beigemessen wird, bildet es das Zentrum des Hauses. Der Westflügel enthält fünf Schlafräume mit drei Bädern, die vor den Schlafzimmern liegen. Der Ostflügel wird fast ganz vom Wohnraum eingenommen, der in drei Bereiche unterteilt ist: Eßplatz und Sitzgruppe, getrennt durch den freistehenden Kamin und das »Musikzimmer«, die Zone um den Konzertflügel. Am Südende dieses Traktes liegt ein kleineres Studio. Die Querspange zwischen den beiden Flügeln nimmt die Küche mit Frühstücksbar auf, die, nur zum Eingang hin durch ein Wandelement geschlossen, zugleich als Passage zwischen Wohn- und Schlafteil dient. Im Eingangsbereich ist die Südfassade des Hauses zurückgenommen, so daß eine Nische entsteht, zu der ein überdachtes Brückendeck führt. Diese Plattform, die auf Stützen in einer Wasserfläche ruht, betritt man von der Seite her über einige Stufen. Der rationalen, streng logischen Gliederung des Grundrisses entspricht die Präzision des konstruktiven Aufbaus. Schlank dimensionierte Stahlstützen tragen die Decken- und Bodenplatte, die vier Stufen über den Erdboden angehoben ist. Eine rings um das Haus geführte Schüttung aus dunklen Kieseln, begrenzt durch einen umlaufenden plattenbelegten Weg, scheint sich unter dem Haus hindurch fortzusetzen. Zusammen mit der Zurücknahme der Fassade hinter die Stützen wird so der Eindruck des Schwebens hervorgerufen. Geschoßhohe, getönte Glasflächen, unterbrochen nur durch wenige Wandfelder aus Pentelikonmarmor, verleihen dem Haus Transparenz. Bodenplatte Gußbeton; Holzflachdach.

4. View from the north side of the living room across the sitting room towards the fireplace and the walnut panelling of the study. The dining area is visible through the fireplace opening. The sitting room and fireplace area is screened from the outside by a large wall panel.

5. Through the room-high glass panels, partly designed as sliding doors, interior and exterior seem to merge and the golf course on the north side of the house appears to be part of the site. The carpets define the different areas of the living room and serve to group the different sets of furniture.

6. Dining area, seen from the kitchen from which it is not physically separated. The light fittings are flush with the ceiling. Outside the sliding door, steps lead to the side courtyard where the site is bordered by a fence.

7. View from the master bedroom towards the golf course. Behind the partition at the head of the beds is the dressing room with built-in cupboards.

4. Blick vom Nordteil des Wohnraums über die Sitzgruppe auf den Kamin und die mit Nußbaumholz verkleidete Wand des Studios. Durch die Feueröffnung des Kamins ist der Eßplatz zu erkennen. Im Bereich der Sitzgruppe und des Kamins ist der Raum gegen außen durch ein großflächiges Wandpanel abgeschirmt.

5. Wandhohe Glasflächen, teilweise als Schiebetüren ausgebildet, lassen Innen- und Außenraum ineinander übergehen: der nach Norden anschließende Golfplatz wird zu einem Teil des Grundstücks. Die Teppiche umschreiben die Bereiche des Wohnraums und fassen die Möbelgruppen zusammen.

6. Der Eßplatz vom Küchenbereich her gesehen, der ohne Raumtrennung anschließt. In der Decke bündig eingelassene Strahler. Von der Schiebetür führt eine Treppe in den seitlichen Hof, wo eine Bretterwand das Grundstück begrenzt.

7. Aus dem Elternschlafraum blickt man auf den Golfplatz. Hinter der Trennwand am Kopfende der Betten liegt die Ankleide mit Einbauschränken.

8. The swimming pool in the centre of the house is level with the ground. In this way, the elevation of the house above the ground has been maintained in the patio as well. Moreover, the windows are protected against splashing water. The pergola slats may later be canopied by glass or plastic.

9, 10. The interlocking of patio, side wings and north terrace, together with the staggered levels and the variety of views across the house, results in endless three-dimensional interplay.

8. Das Schwimmbecken im Zentrum des Hauses liegt niveaugleich mit dem Grundstücksterrain. Damit wird auch im Bereich des Atriums die Abhebung des Baukörpers vom Erdboden beibehalten; außerdem sind damit die Glasflächen vor Wasserspritzern geschützt. Die Lamellen der Pergola sollen später mit einer Glas- oder Kunststoffhaut abgedeckt werden.

9, 10. Das Ineinandergreifen von Atrium, Seitenflügeln und Nordterrasse ergibt mit der Höhenstufung und den vielfältigen Durchblicken ein reiches räumliches Beziehungsspiel.

11. The corner view of the east and north sides clearly demonstrates the strict symmetry of the entire design.

12. The symmetrical design also includes the car port and bridge deck on the south side.

11. In der Übereck-Ansicht der Ost- und Nordseite wird die strenge Symmetrie der Gesamtanlage deutlich.

12. Auch Wageneinstellplatz und Zugangsdeck auf der Südseite sind in die Symmetrie einbezogen.

1. North side. The entrance is screened by a precast concrete screen to ensure privacy and shelter from the wind. On the left is the access road with the entrance to the ground floor garage.
2. It is only on the south side that the house opens up. The trees in the garden help to ensure sun protection and privacy.
3. A view of the hall. The asbestos-cement sheeting of the party wall behind the mirror is identical with that used outside.

1. Blick von Norden. Vor dem Eingang eine Betonblende als Sicht- und Windschutz. Links die Zufahrtsstraße und die Einfahrt zur Garage im Erdgeschoß.
2. Nur auf der Südseite öffnet sich das Haus zur Außenwelt. Die Bäume im Garten geben Sonnen- und Sichtschutz.
3. Blick in die Diele. Die Fassadenverkleidung aus Asbestzementplatten kehrt an der Innenwand hinter dem Spiegel wieder.

Architect's house at Lauttasaari, near Helsinki
Architect: Toivo Korhonen. Associate: Jaakko Laapotti

With this house, the architect Toivo Korhonen intended to create, for his family of four, the background for an extremely private and secluded life. In the setting of a rather densely populated suburban area, he regarded a courtyard-type house as the most sensible solution. Except on the south side, the square two-storey building is almost entirely enclosed. The severe facade, clad with white asbestos-cement sheets, is only broken by a narrow strip of windows. The impression of seclusion is further reinforced by the solid precast concrete screen surrounding the garden. The sober external appearance is matched by the consistent adherence to a strict module in the plan. All the rooms are grouped around the courtyard overlooking it with storey-high windows. On the upper floor, the entire west side is taken up by the living room which is divided into three areas, the dining area at the north end, the sitting area near the fireplace and, beyond a sliding partition, the library. In the opposite wing are, from south to north, the master bedroom, two children's bedrooms, a guest room and a studio, separated by three shower rooms, with W.C.s. The bedroom corridor can be closed by sliding doors so that the whole bedroom wing can be separated from the rest of the house. On the north side, the two wings are connected by the kitchen which is flanked by two flights of stairs leading to the ground floor. Between kitchen and courtyard is a breakfast area. On the south side, stairs lead from the courtyard to the garden. In the recessed ground floor are a swimming pool, sauna, a large hobby room, two staff rooms and a garage. Construction: Ground floor: Concrete. Upper floor: Wood post-and-beam structure placed on a cantilevered reinforced concrete slab. Prefabricated wall panels, faced on the outside with asbestos-cement sheets and on the inside with polished plywood. Wood batten ceiling. Mosaic tile flooring. Floor heating.

Architektenhaus in Lauttasaari bei Helsinki
Architekt: Toivo Korhonen. Mitarbeiter: Jaakko Laapotti

Mit diesem Haus wollte der Architekt Toivo Korhonen seiner vierköpfigen Familie den Rahmen für ein im höchsten Maße privates und zurückgezogenes Leben schaffen. Diesen sah er innerhalb der relativ dichten Vorstadtbebauung am zweckmäßigsten durch ein Atriumhaus gegeben. Das quadratische, zweigeschossige Gebäude ist nach außen, mit Ausnahme der Südseite, fast völlig geschlossen. Nur ein schmales Fensterband lockert die strenge, mit weißen Asbestzementplatten verkleidete Fassade auf. Der Eindruck des Sich-Abschließens wird noch verstärkt durch die Umfriedung des Gartens mit großen, vorgefertigten Betonelementen. Der nüchternen Gestaltung des Außenbaues entspricht der strenge, einem konsequent durchgehaltenen Rastermaß folgende Grundriß. Alle Räume sind um das Atrium gruppiert, auf das sie sich durch geschoßhohe Fensterwände öffnen. Die ganze Westseite nimmt der Wohnteil ein, der in drei Zonen unterteilt wurde: am Nordende der Eßplatz, daran anschließend der eigentliche Wohnbereich, begrenzt durch Kamin und Wandscheibe, hinter der als dritte Zone die Bibliothek liegt. Im gegenüberliegenden Hausflügel befinden sich, von Süden nach Norden, Elternschlafraum, zwei Kinderzimmer, Gästezimmer und Studio. In diese Raumfolge sind drei Duschräume mit WC eingeschoben. Der davorliegende Umgang läßt sich durch Schiebetüren abschließen, so daß der Schlafbereich der Familie von den übrigen Hausteilen abgetrennt werden kann. Die Verbindung zwischen den beiden Flügeln stellt auf der Nordseite die Küche her. Sie ist von zwei Treppen flankiert, die ins Erdgeschoß führen. Zwischen Küche und Atrium liegt ein zweiter, für den internen Familiengebrauch bestimmter Eßplatz. Auf der Südseite verbindet eine Treppe das Atrium mit dem Hausgarten. Im zurückgesetzten Erdgeschoß befinden sich Schwimmbecken, Sauna und ein großer Hobbyraum; außerdem die Wohnräume der beiden Dienstboten und die Garage. Konstruktion: Erdgeschoß Beton. Obergeschoß Holzständer-Fachwerk auf auskragender Stahlbetondecke. Vorgefertigte Wandelemente, außen mit Asbestzementplatten, innen mit furnierten Spanplatten verkleidet. Holzlamellendecke. Fußboden mit Kunststeinplatten belegt. Fußbodenheizung.

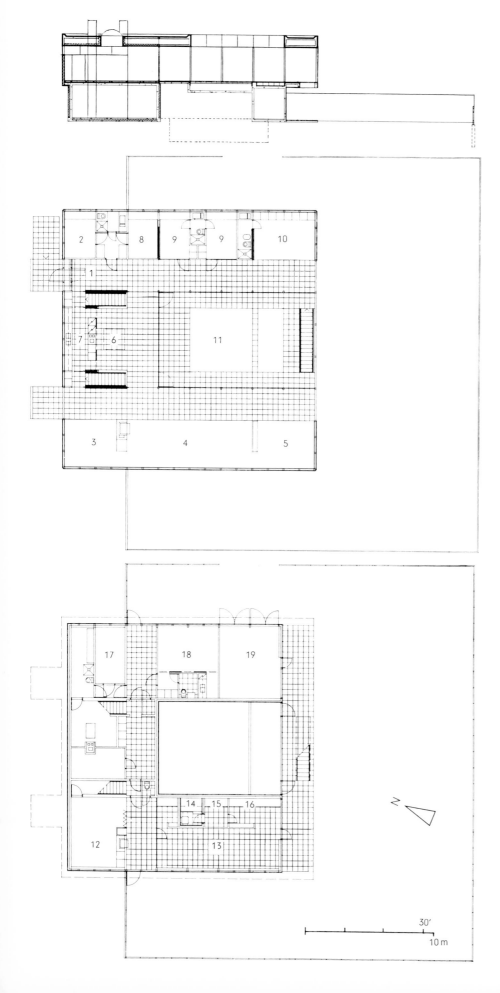

30'

10 m

4. Section and plan of upper floor and ground floor (bottom). Key: 1 entrance and hall, 2 studio, 3 dining area, 4 living room, 5 library, 6 breakfast area, 7 kitchen, 8 guest room, 9 children's bedroom, 10 master bedroom, 11 courtyard, 12 hobby room, 13 swimming pool, 14 sauna, 15 laundry, 16 dressing room, 17 maid's room, 18 caretaker, 19 garage.

5. A view towards the living room which can be separated from the hall by a sliding door. In the foreground on the right is the breakfast area with top lighting; on the left, the window facing the courtyard is just visible. The light fittings are flush with the wood batten ceiling.

4. Schnitt und Grundrisse von Obergeschoß und Erdgeschoß (unten). Legende: 1 Eingang und Diele, 2 Studio, 3 Eßplatz, 4 Wohnraum, 5 Bibliothek, 6 Zweiter Eßplatz, 7 Küche, 8 Gastzimmer, 9 Kinderzimmer, 10 Elternschlafraum, 11 Atrium, 12 Hobbyraum, 13 Schwimmbecken, 14 Sauna, 15 Waschraum, 16 Umkleidezimmer, 17 Mädchenzimmer, 18 Hausmeister, 19 Garage.

5. Blick in den Wohnraum, der durch eine Schiebetür zur Diele hin geschlossen werden kann. Rechts im Vordergrund der familieninterne Eßplatz mit Oberlicht, links angeschnitten die Fensterwand zum Atrium. In der Holzlamellendecke eingelassene Leuchtwannen.

6. Living room, seen from the fireplace. Behind the partition is the library zone. On the left, one of the two doors leading to the courtyard.
7. Chairs and table in the library zone. The large south windows have sun blinds instead of curtains.

6. Blick vom Kamin in den Wohnraum. Hinter der querstehenden Wandscheibe der Bibliotheksbereich. Links eine der beiden Türen zum Atrium.
7. Sitzgruppe in der Bibliothek. Die großen Südfenster haben Jalousien anstelle von Vorhängen.

8. Parents' bedroom. The beds can be curtained off on the courtyard side.

9, 10. All the rooms face the courtyard which can be seen from any point inside the house. This also helps to offset any sense of confinement.

11. South side of the house with the stairs leading to the upper floor. The toplight windows create an horizontal extension of the main windows.

12. Ground floor swimming pool, with the hobby room in the background.

8. Blick in den Elternschlafraum. Die Bettenkoje

läßt sich durch einen Vorhang gegen das Atrium schließen.

9, 10. Alle Räume sind zum Atrium hin orientiert, das von jedem Punkt im Innern des Hauses sichtbar ist. Es wird damit auch der Eindruck räumlicher Enge vermieden.

11. Südansicht des Hauses mit der Treppe zum Obergeschoß. Die Oberlichter der Fenster sind so bemessen, daß sie optisch das umlaufende Fensterband fortführen.

12. Das Schwimmbecken im Untergeschoß. Dahinter der Hobbyraum.

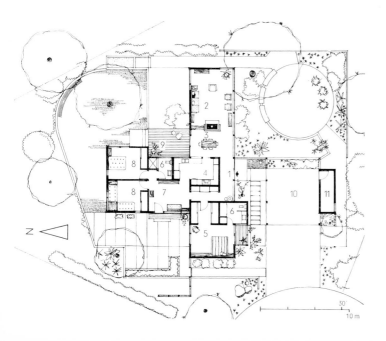

1. West side with drive, car port and entrance. On the left is the wing with the parents' bedroom and the dark-glazed sundeck. The play garden is screened by a fence.
2. Plan. Key: 1 entrance and hall, 2 living room, 3 dining area, 4 kitchen, 5 master bedroom, 6 bathroom and shower, 7 activity room, 8 children's bedroom, 9 sundeck, 10 car port, 11 storage room.

1. Blick von Westen auf Zufahrt, Wageneinstellplatz und Eingang. Links der Flügel für die Eltern mit der durch Glasblenden geschützten Sonnenterrasse. Eine Bretterwand schirmt den Spielgarten ab.
2. Grundriß. Legende: 1 Eingang und Diele, 2 Wohnraum, 3 Eßplatz, 4 Küche, 5 Elternschlafraum, 6 Bad, Dusche, 7 Activity-Raum, 8 Kinderzimmer, 9 Sonnenterrasse, 10 Wageneinstellplatz, 11 Abstellraum.

3. A view of the living room in the column-borne south wing. Below it is the concrete paved circular patio.

4. View from north-east with living room wing (left) and children's wing (right). At the intersection point is the sundeck outside the dining area. The play garden is bordered by a low wall.

3. Ansicht des auf Stützen stehenden, nach Süden orientierten Wohnflügels. Davor die kreisförmige, zementierte Arena.

4. Blick von Nordosten auf Wohnflügel (links) und Kinderflügel (rechts). Im Schnittpunkt die Terrasse vor dem Eßplatz. Der Spielgarten wird durch eine niedrige Mauer begrenzt.

Architect's house at Santa Barbara, California
Architect: Robert S. Grant

The site, sloping downward at a 1 in 5 gradient towards the south-east, is embellished by old eucalyptus trees and enjoys a fine view of city and ocean. The family of five wanted a house offering plenty of scope for outdoor activities. For this reason an individual outdoor space has been assigned to each group of rooms: thus, the playground garden on the north side to the children's domain; the circular patio in the south-east corner to the living room, and a sundeck each to the dining area and the main bedroom. The plan is reminiscent of a windmill with wings of unequal length, reaching out to the four directions of the compass. In the south wing are a car port and storage room, in the west wing the master bedroom with bathroom and dressing room. The north wing is reserved to the children, and the east wing contains the living room and dining area. In the centre of the house is the kitchen with the adjacent 'activity room' which serves as a place for television, games and hobbies and can be easily supervised from the kitchen. Towards the road, the house is completely enclosed. It is only through the car port that a glimpse can be had of the garden. The isolated position of the master bedroom ensures privacy and quiet, and the privacy of the sundeck in front of the south window is ensured by storey-high darkened glass panes. Construction: Wood post-and-beam structure on concrete blocks. Wooden roof, Douglas fir decking. Interior and exterior walls are plastered. Warm air heating.

Architektenhaus in Santa Barbara, California
Architekt: Robert S. Grant

Dem Grundstück, das sich mit einem Gefälle von etwa 20 % nach Südosten neigt, geben alte Eukalyptusbäume und der Blick auf Stadt und Ozean seinen besonderen Reiz. Die fünfköpfige Familie wünschte sich ein Haus, das vielfältige Möglichkeiten bietet, im Freien zu leben. Deshalb ist jeder Raumgruppe eine Freifläche zugeordnet: der Spielgarten auf der Nordseite den Kinderzimmern, der kreisförmige Sitzplatz in der Südostecke dem Wohnraum, und Eßplatz wie auch Schlafraum je ein Sonnendeck. Der Grundriß gleicht einer Windmühle mit ungleich langen Flügeln, die nach den vier Himmelsrichtungen ausgreifen. Der Südflügel umfaßt Wageneinstellplatz und Abstellraum, der Westflügel den Elternschlafraum mit Bad und Ankleide. Der Nordflügel ist den Kindern vorbehalten, und im Ostflügel sind Wohnraum und Eßplatz untergebracht. Im Zentrum des Hauses liegt die Küche mit dem angrenzenden Activity-Raum, der als Fernseh-, Spiel- und Hobbyzimmer dient und von der Küche aus leicht zu übersehen ist. Zur Straße hin ist das Haus geschlossen. Nur über den Wageneinstellplatz bietet sich ein Blick in den Garten. Die separate Lage des Elternschlafraumes sichert Ruhe und Abgeschlossenheit. Konstruktion: Holzskelett auf Zementblocksteinen. Holzflachdach innen mit Holzriemen verschalt. Wände verputzt. Warmluftheizung.

5. The entrance, situated between car port and kitchen close to the centre of the house, is sympathetically designed with pools of water and plants, stepping stones and an open roof. The privacy of the living room is ensured by a grille.
6. Master bedroom. Behind the glass sliding door is the sundeck, adjacent to it the bathroom, and on the left the dressing room with built-in cupboards.

5. Der mit Wasser- und Pflanzenbecken, Trittsteinen und Lichtöffnung im Dach liebevoll gestaltete Eingang liegt zwischen Wageneinstellplatz und Küche etwa in der Mitte des Hauses. Ein Lattenrost schützt die Fenster des Wohnraums gegen Einblick.
6. Blick in das Elternschlafzimmer. Hinter der Glasschiebetür die Sonnenterrasse, anschließend das Bad und links der Ankleideraum mit eingebauten Schränken, über den man den Elternschlafraum betritt.

7–9. Dining area and living room form an entity, subdivided by fireplace and cupboard unit and reaching out with passages to hall, kitchen and sundeck.

7–9. Eßplatz und Wohnraum bilden eine Einheit, die durch den Kamin und ein Schrankelement optisch unterteilt wird. Mit Durchgängen zu Diele, Küche und Sonnendeck greift der Raum weiter aus.

Architect's house at Karlsruhe, Germany
Architect: Reinhard Gieselmann

1. General view from the south, with the black box-like superstructure of the studio gallery.
2. Office block and the architect's own office; beneath it the entrance to the residence. In the architect's own words: 'The shapes are despoiled cubes and disfigured faces, lacerated or serrated corners, dilapidated rectangles, rhythms against and with the slope, interlocking volumes, and projections; a complete revolt of the shapes against the perfection of the pure rectangle.'
3. Stairs leading from the ground floor to the secretary's office.

1. Gesamtansicht von Süden mit dem schwarzen, kastenförmigen Aufsatz der Ateliergalerie.
2. Büroblock und Chefbüro, darunter der Eingang zum Wohnhaus. »Die Formen«, sagt der Architekt, »sind versehrte Kuben und verletzte Flächen..., aufgelöste oder ausgezahnte Ecken, verfremdete Rechtecke, Rhythmen gegen den Hang und mit dem Hang, Verklammerungen der Volumen und Auskragungen: ein ganzer Formen-Aufstand gegen die Perfektion des reinen Rechtecks.«
3. Aufgang vom Erdgeschoß zum Sekretariat.

The design of this group of buildings has developed from the specific requirements which arose when the architect designed his own house and studio. He wanted not only a home for his family but also office accommodation for himself and his assistants, connected with the house yet with a clear segregation between private and business activities. He also wanted to include living accommodation for his assistants, so that the programme comprised three further dwelling units, a bachelor's flat and two three room flats. All the dwellings were to be given maximum privacy compatible with the intended architectural arrangement, by providing separate entrances and gardens so that each individual dwelling had its private open space. The house stands at the edge of the town on sloping ground, which used to be a vineyard and falls steeply towards south. The group comprises three buildings which surround a central courtyard. Seven of the nine levels are adapted to the slope and provide direct ground level exit. Closest to the road on the valley side is the office building which contains three garages in its ground floor, and the studio with a superimposed gallery floor, on the upper levels. The secretary's office is next to the drawing office and forms the entrance to the architect's own office which is placed a few steps higher and has a direct entrance from the two-storey residence as well. The main entrance of the residence leads through the ground floor hall via a flight of stairs to the central living room. Behind the hall are a guest room, the boiler room and basements. Grouped around the living room are dining area, kitchen, boudoir and, a few steps higher, a small sitting room which, like the hall, faces onto a terrace. It is reached via the lower steps of the spiral stairs which lead up to the bedroom floor where the three bedrooms are grouped around a roof terrace. The central patio, directly accessible from the living room, is bordered on the west side by the two upper floors of the blocks of flats. Construction: load-bearing walls and structural floors of concrete. Boarded ceilings; wood and stone floors.

Architektenhaus in Karlsruhe, Deutschland
Architekt: Reinhard Gieselmann

Dieser Gebäudekomplex ist konsequent aus den speziellen Bedürfnissen und Notwendig-keiten entwickelt, die sich ergaben, als der Architekt sein eigenes Wohnhaus mit ange-schlossenem Atelier plante. Er hatte nicht nur Wohnraum für seine Familie zu schaffen, sondern auch Büroräume für sich und seine Mitarbeiter, wobei Wohnung und Büro zwar miteinander verbunden sein sollten, aber doch eine klare Trennung zwischen privater und geschäftlicher Sphäre erstrebt wurde. Außerdem lag es nahe, auch für die Mitarbeiter geeigneten Wohnraum zu schaffen. So umfaßt das Raumprogramm noch drei weitere Wohneinheiten: ein Junggesellenapartment und zwei Dreieinhalb-Zimmer-Wohnungen. Alle Wohnungen sollten ein Maximum an Abgeschlossenheit erhalten, soweit dies innerhalb der beabsichtigten architektonischen Ordnung möglich war. Eigener Eingang und eigenes Gärtchen und damit die Anbindung jeder einzelnen Wohnung an privaten Freiraum sollten dazu beitragen. Das Haus steht auf einem Hanggrundstück am Stadtrand, das früher als Weinberg genutzt wurde und steil nach Süden fällt. Der Baukörper ist in drei Kuben aufge-löst, die um einen in der Mitte liegenden Hof angeordnet wurden. Sieben von neun Ebenen sind an den Hang angeglichen und haben einen direkten Ausgang ins Freie. Zur talseitigen Straße vorgeschoben ist der Büroblock, der im Erdgeschoß drei Garagen aufnimmt; darüber liegt das Atelier mit einem aufgesetzten Galeriegeschoß. Das Sekretariat neben dem Zeichensaal leitet über zu dem einige Stufen höher liegenden Chefbüro, das als Zwischen-glied die Verbindung zum zweigeschossigen Wohnhaus des Architekten herstellt. Der direkte Zugang zu seiner Wohnung führt durch die Diele im Erdgeschoß, hinter der ein Gastzimmer, die Heizung und Kellerräume liegen, über eine Treppe in die zentrale Wohn-halle. Um diese gruppieren sich Eßplatz, Küche, Zimmer der Dame und um einige Stufen angehoben der kleine Wohnraum. Er wird über die untersten Stufen der Wendeltreppe er-schlossen, die in das Schlafgeschoß mit drei Räumen rings um eine Dachterrasse führt. Der zentrale Innenhof ist von der Wohnhalle aus zugänglich. Konstruktion: Tragende Wände und Geschoßdecken Beton. Decken holzverschalt, Böden Holz und Stein.

4

4. This general view from south-east clearly shows how the whole building complex is adapted to the different levels of the slope. White plaster; base and apertures black; shutters in pale grass green.

5. Plans. From left to right: ground floor, first floor and second floor. Key: 1 entrance to the residence, with hall, 2 guest room, 3 heating, 4 basement, 5 entrance to office and flats, 6 office model room, 7 bachelor's flat, 8 tenants' basements, 9 garage, 10 three room flat, 11 studio, 12 secretary's office, 13 architect's own office, 14 living room, 15 dining area, 16 kitchen, 17 boudoir, 18 small sitting room, 19 studio gallery, 20 bedroom, 21 roof terrace.

6. Studio. The strip of windows directly above the drawing boards face west and south. On the high-level gallery, which receives daylight from the north, there is space for two further desks suspended from the ceiling.

7. Living room. In the background, the window front facing the east terrace. On the right, the fireside corner.

8. Spiral stairs leading to the bedroom floor and to the small sitting room which is five steps above the living room proper. On the left the passage to the boudoir.

9. Dining area with hatch from the kitchen; the large floor to ceiling windows on the left face the central courtyard.

4. Die Gesamtansicht von Südosten macht deutlich, wie sich der Komplex in verschiedenen Stufen dem Hang anpaßt. Putz weiß, Sockel und Öffnungen schwarz, Rolläden in verwaschenem Grasgrün.

5. Grundrisse. Von links nach rechts: Erdgeschoß, erstes Obergeschoß und zweites Obergeschoß. Legende: 1 Eingang zum Wohnhaus und Diele, 2 Gastzimmer, 3 Heizung, 4 Keller, 5 Eingang zum Büro und den Mietwohnungen, 6 Bastelraum Büro, 7 Junggesellenwohnung, 8 Keller Mietwohnungen, 9 Garage, 10 Dreieinhalb-Zimmer-Wohnung, 11 Atelier, 12 Sekretariat, 13 Chefbüro, 14 Wohnhalle, 15 Eßplatz, 16 Küche, 17 Zimmer der Dame, 18 Kleiner Wohnraum,

5

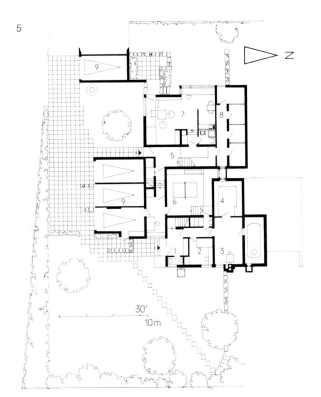

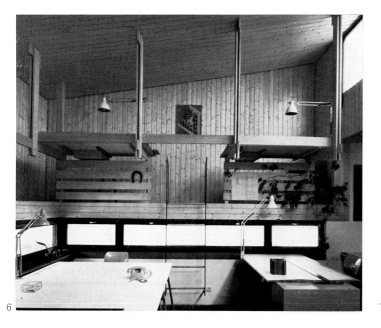

6

7

19 Galerie Atelier, 20 Schlafraum, 21 Dachterrasse.
6. Blick in das Atelier mit dem nach Westen und
Süden gerichteten Fensterband über den Zei-
chentischen und der aufgesetzten Galerie, die
von Norden belichtet wird und Platz für zwei
weitere, von der Decke abgehängte Arbeits-
plätze bietet.
7. Blick in die Wohnhalle mit der Fensterwand
zur Ostterrasse und der Sitzgruppe am Kamin.
8. Wendeltreppe zum Schlafgeschoß und dem
fünf Stufen höher liegenden kleinen Wohnraum.
Links Durchgang zum Zimmer der Dame.
9. Eßplatz mit Durchreiche zur Küche; links die
Fensterwand zum zentralen Hof.

8

9

Architect's house at Cedar Rapids, Iowa
Architects: Ray D. Crites and R. D. McConnell

The site is part of an extensive wooded and undulating area at the east edge of Cedar Rapids where the same architects were also responsible for the design of the Shuttleworth House (page 120). R.D. Crites' house was placed on the highest point of the site so as to provide the best possible view despite the proximity of the trees. This situation, together with the specific wishes of the family of five, led the architects to adopt a development in height. Each area of activity was assigned to a different storey, resulting in a four-storey building where, in accordance with the occupiers' wishes, every room has a terrace or balcony. As the parents wanted their sleeping areas to be well away from those of the children, the master bedroom is placed on the top floor whilst the three bedrooms of the children are on the floor below. They are placed along the three sides of the upper space of the two-storey portion of the living room, and are accessible from a gallery. Most of the upper ground floor level is taken up by the 50 ft. long, living room which is divided into four areas (dining, fireside, and two groups of chairs and tables) by a cupboard unit, by the island-type fireplace, and by changes in the levels of floors and ceilings. Construction: timber framing, with cedar wood boarding inside and out. Lower floor walls and columns of concrete.

Architektenhaus in Cedar Rapids, Iowa
Architekten: Ray D. Crites und R. D. McConnell

Das Grundstück gehört zu einem ausgedehnten, bewaldeten und stark gewellten Baugelände am Ostrand von Cedar Rapids, auf dem die Architekten auch das Haus Shuttleworth (Seite 120) errichteten. Das Gebäude wurde auf dem höchsten Punkt des Areals erstellt, um trotz der dicht heranrückenden Bäume einen gewissen Ausblick zu ermöglichen. Diese Situation und die fest umrissenen Wohnvorstellungen der fünfköpfigen Familie Crites ließen die Architekten das Raumprogramm vertikal abwickeln. Den einzelnen Wohnbereichen wurde jeweils ein Stockwerk zugewiesen, so daß sich ein viergeschossiger Bau ergab, der es erlaubte, wie gewünscht jedem Raum eine Terrasse oder einen Balkon zuzuordnen. Da der Schlafbereich der Eltern von dem der Kinder getrennt werden sollte, liegt der Elternschlafraum im obersten, dem zweiten Obergeschoß und die drei Kinderzimmer ein Stockwerk tiefer. Sie gruppieren sich auf drei Seiten um den oberen Teil des an dieser Stelle zweigeschossigen Wohnraums und werden über eine Galerie erschlossen. Das ebenerdige Hauptgeschoß wird großenteils von dem rund fünfzehn Meter langen Wohnraum eingenommen. Ein raumteilendes Schrankelement, der frei stehende Kamin und unterschiedliche Boden- und Deckenhöhen gliedern ihn in vier Zonen: Eßplatz, Sitzplatz, Kaminbereich und zweite Sitzgruppe. Holzständerkonstruktion, innen und außen mit Zedernholzschalung. Im Untergeschoß Wände und Stützen aus Beton.

1. View from the south into the corner formed by the transverse (kitchen) wing and the longitudinal main wing which cascades down from the level of the master bedroom to the car port at ground level. The contrasted yet disciplined grouping of towers of different heights, loosely inter-connected, and separated by large areas. The sculptural effect is further enhanced by overhanging balconies where the horizontal accent is, however, offset somewhat by the vertical motif of the wooden slat balustrades.
2. The storey-and-a-half portion of the living room, projecting northwards, is set on columns.
3. Seen from the roof terrace above the car port, the step-like rise of the towers is particularly evident. On the left is the kitchen and, above it, one of the children's rooms.

1. Blick von Süden in den Winkel zwischen Küchen-, Quer- und Längstrakt, der sich von der Höhe des Elternschlafraums bis herunter zum Wageneinstellplatz abtreppt. Lebhaft bewegte, aber doch disziplinierte Gruppierung von verschieden hohen Türmen in lockerem Verbund, getrennt durch große Glasflächen. Zusätzliche Bereicherung des plastischen Volumens durch auskragende Balkone, deren Horizontalität jedoch durch die Vertikaltendenz der Lattenbrüstungen überlagert wird.
2. Der nach Norden vorgeschobene, eineinhalbgeschossige Teil des Wohnraums ist auf Stützen gestellt.
3. Von der Dachterrasse über dem Wageneinstellplatz aus wird das stufenweise Ansteigen der Turmelemente besonders deutlich. Links die Küche und darüber ein Kinderzimmer.

150

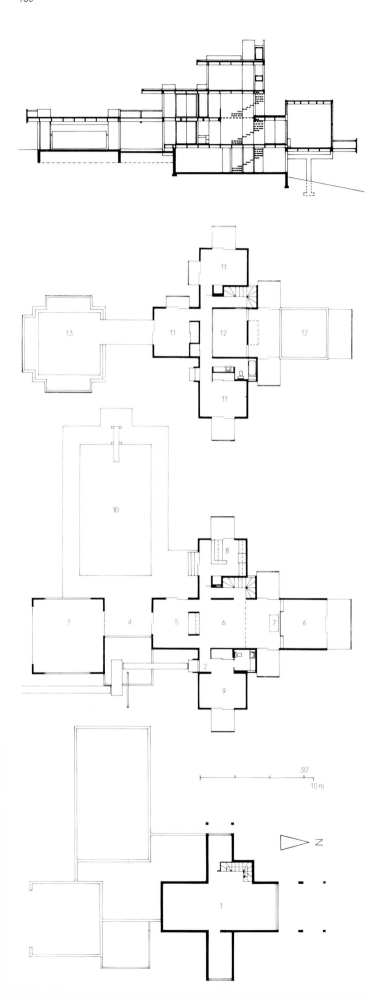

4. Longitudinal section and plans. From bottom to top: lower ground floor, upper ground floor, first floor and second floor (right). Key: 1 hobby room, 2 entrance, 3 car port, 4 dining terrace, 5 dining area, 6 living room, 7 fireside area, 8 kitchen, 9 study, 10 swimming pool (future), 11 children's room, 12 upper space of living room, 13 sundeck, 14 master bedroom.
5. Perspective drawing of the view from the north.

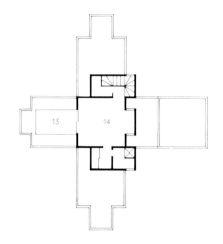

4. Längsschnitt und Grundrisse. Von unten nach oben: Untergeschoß, Erdgeschoß, 1. und 2. Obergeschoß (rechts). Legende: 1 Hobbyraum, 2 Eingang, 3 Wageneinstellplatz, 4 Eßterrasse, 5 Eßplatz, 6 Wohnraum, 7 Kaminbereich, 8 Küche, 9 Studio, 10 Geplantes Schwimmbecken, 11 Kinderzimmer, 12 Luftraum Wohnraum, 13 Sonnendeck, 14 Elternschlafraum.
5. Perspektive; Ansicht von Norden.

6. View from the sundeck above the car port towards the bedrooms. Those of the children are at sundeck level; the master bedroom is on the upper floor and is dominated by the stair and service towers. Apart from minor details, the overall design is strictly symmetrical.

7. The view in the opposite direction, as seen from the master bedroom, shows the children's sundeck and the driveway. The plankway on the left forms a footpath to the house entrance.

6. Blick vom Sonnendeck über dem Wageneinstellplatz auf das Schlafgeschoß der Kinder und das darüberliegende Elternschlafzimmer, das von dem Treppenhausturm und dem Installationsturm überragt wird. Bis auf kleine Abweichungen ist die Gesamtanlage streng symmetrisch.

7. In der Gegenrichtung bietet sich vom Elternschlafraum aus der Blick auf das Sonnendeck der Kinder und die Zufahrt. Links ein Brettersteg, der zum Hauseingang führt.

8–10. Different views of the living room. Top left: low-ceilinged fireside area, seen from the projecting northern part of the living room which is one step lower and extends through one-and-a-half storeys. Behind the fireplace is the low-ceilinged lounge, above it the gallery to the children's bedrooms. The cupboard unit which segregates the dining area is visible behind the fireplace cowl. Top right: view in the opposite direction. Bottom: the one-and-a-half storey rooms have full-height windows.

8–10. Ansichten des Wohnraums. Oben links: Durchblick aus dem eineinhalbgeschossigen, eine Stufe tiefer liegenden Wohnbereich im auskragenden Nordteil auf den Kaminbereich mit tiefgezogener Decke. Dahinter die Sitzgruppe im zweigeschossigen Teil mit der Galerie zu den Kinderzimmern. Neben der Kaminhaube ist das raumteilende Schrankelement zum Eßplatz hin zu erkennen. Oben rechts: Blick in der Gegenrichtung. Unten: Der anderthalbgeschossige Wohnteil ist zum Balkon in voller Höhe verglast.

11, 12. Two further views of the living room which forms the two-storey centre of the house. The vertical motif of the balcony balustrades is repeated at the indoor gallery and again at the stairs landing. The space above the low ceiling of the side area is visible through the window on the right.

13. One of the three children's bedrooms on the first floor. The passage on the left leads to the sundeck.

14. The L-shaped breakfast table in the kitchen is built around the island-type sink.

11, 12. Zwei weitere Ansichten aus dem Wohnraum, dem zweigeschossigen Zentrum des Hauses. Das Motiv der Balkongitter ist an der Galerie im Innenraum wieder aufgegriffen; auch am Podest des Treppenhauses tritt es auf. Durch das Fenster rechts davon blickt man über das tiefgezogene Dach des Kaminbereiches.

13. Eines der drei Kinderzimmer im ersten Obergeschoß. Links der Durchgang zum Sonnendeck.

14. Der winkelförmige Frühstücksplatz in der Küche ist an den Spültisch angebaut.

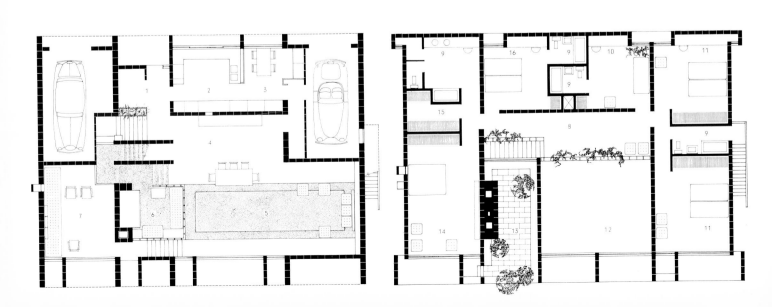

House for A. W. Milam, St. John's County, Jacksonville, Florida
Architect: Paul Rudolph

This house stands on sand dunes on the Atlantic coast, some 46 ft. above the high-water mark and is built of beige-coloured concrete blocks. The structure is not designed to any modular system.

The facade is dominated by an irregular network of horizontal and vertical screens. The variegated 'mesh' they form is an outward expression of the irregular plan and arrangement of the rooms. All the areas of the living room merge. They are spread over several levels, and it is these changes in level in conjunction with the different ceiling heights which define the boundaries of the different areas. The core, and at the same time the lowest level, is formed by the oblong sitting pit set behind the windows facing the Atlantic. Adjacent to the narrow side of this pit, but separated from it by a low balustrade, is the fireside area which is six steps higher and reached via the intermediate level of the dining area (placed at the inside extension of the upper edge of the pit). The ceiling is of about normal height above the table end of the pit, but is raised to twice this height above the other half, dropping again above the fireside area to an intermediate height somewhat higher than that of the gallery above the dining area. The robust fireside unit forms a screen between the living area proper and the children's playroom which is on the lowest level of the house and has a separate entrance. Master bedroom, guest room, staff and children's bedrooms, each with bathroom and W. C., are on the upper floor.

Haus A. W. Milam, St. John's County, Jacksonville, Florida
Architekt: Paul Rudolph

Ein unregelmäßiges Netz horizontaler und vertikaler Blenden vor der Wohnfront, in dessen unterschiedlich großen »Maschen« die Vielgestaltigkeit der Grundriß- und Raumgliederung anklingt, bestimmt das Gesicht dieses Hauses. Alle Bereiche des Wohnteiles fließen ineinander. Sie sind auf mehrere Ebenen verteilt, deren Versetzung gegeneinander zusammen mit unterschiedlichen Deckenhöhen die Raumgrenzen umschreibt. Kernbereich und zugleich tiefste Ebene ist die langgestreckte, rechteckige Sitzgrube hinter der dem Atlantik zugekehrten Fensterfront. An die Schmalseite dieser Sitzgrube schließt sich, getrennt durch eine niedrige Balustrade, der sechs Stufen höher liegende Kaminplatz an, den man über die Zwischenebene des Eßplatzes – auf der Fortsetzung des oberen Randes der Sitzgrube zum Hausinnern hin – erreicht. Die Decke springt von etwa Normalgeschoßhöhe über dem Couchtisch der Sitzgrube auf doppelte Raumhöhe über der anschließenden Hälfte und ist über dem Kaminsitzplatz wieder auf eine Zwischenstufe abgesenkt die jedoch noch etwas höher liegt als die Galerie über dem Eßplatz. Der kräftige Kaminblock schirmt den Wohnbereich gegen das Kinderspielzimmer auf der tiefsten Ebene des Hauses ab, das einen gesonderten Zugang hat. Elternschlafraum, Gastzimmer, Mädchen- und Kinderzimmer, jeweils mit Bad und WC, befinden sich im Obergeschoß. Das Haus steht auf den Sanddünen der Atlantikküste, etwa 14 Meter über der Flutgrenze. Es ist aus beigefarbenen Betonformsteinen gemauert. Die Konstruktion folgt keinerlei Modularsystem. Alle Räume sind vollklimatisiert.

1. Main front of the house. In the centre is the living room, on the left is the children's playroom and above it the master bedroom; in the top right-hand corner is another children's room. The strict geometrical shapes of the sun screens protecting the facade are in stark contrast to the gently undulating lines of the surrounding dunes.
2. Ground floor plan (left) and upper floor plan. Key: 1 entrance and hall, 2 kitchen, 3 breakfast area, 4 dining area, 5 sitting pit, 6 fireside area, 7 children's playroom, 8 gallery, 9 bathroom, 10 maid's room, 11 children's room, 12 space above sitting room, 13 roof terrace, 14 master bedroom, 15 walk-in cupboard, 16 guest room.
3. Site plan.
4. Longitudinal section of living room zone.

1. Blick auf die Wohnfront des Hauses. In der Mitte der Wohnbereich, links das Kinderspielzimmer mit dem darüberliegenden Elternschlafraum, rechts oben ein Kinderzimmer. Die geometrisch strengen Formen des Sonnenschutzrasters vor der Fassade bilden einen kräftigen Kontrast zu den sanften geschwungenen Linien der Dünen, in denen das Haus steht.
2. Grundrisse von Erdgeschoß (links) und Obergeschoß. Legende: 1 Eingang und Diele, 2 Küche, 3 Frühstücksplatz, 4 Eßplatz, 5 Sitzgrube, 6 Kaminsitzplatz, 7 Kinderspielzimmer, 8 Galerie, 9 Bad, 10 Mädchenzimmer, 11 Kinderzimmer, 12 Luftraum Wohnraum, 13 Dachterrasse, 14 Elternschlafraum, 15 Schrankraum, 16 Gastzimmer.
3. Lageplan.
4. Längsschnitt durch den Wohnbereich.

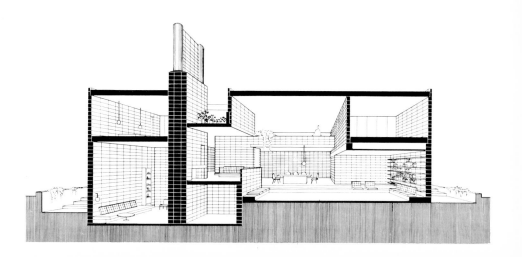

5. A view of the almost windowless entrance side. The facade recesses at ground floor level and at the upper floor windows repeat the sun screen motif of the main front. Behind the blind is the kitchen, to the right of it the entrance recess and to the left of it, behind the storey-high window, the breakfast area.

6. From the dining area and the sitting pit, there is a wide view of the Atlantic. On the right is the brick wall marking the boundary of the fireside area.

7, 8. The sitting pit seen from the fireside lounge (Fig. 7) and vice versa. The living area is sparsely furnished in order to avoid, as far as possible, any visual break in the continuity of the room. The necessary cupboard space is built-in. The partition of the large windows repeats the subdivision of the rooms; the height of the clerestory window corresponds to the vertical distance between gallery balustrade and ceiling.

5. Ansicht der weitgehend geschlossenen Zu-
gangsseite. Die Fassadenrücksprünge im Bereich
des Erdgeschosses und vor den Fenstern des
Obergeschosses wiederholen motivisch den
Blendenraster vor der Wohnfront. Hinter dem
Screen liegt die Küche, rechts davon die Ein-
gangsnische und links davon, hinter dem geschoßhohen Fenster, der Frühstücksplatz.
6. Vom Eßplatz und aus der Sitzgrube blickt man
weit über den Atlantik. Rechts die den Kaminplatz abschließende gemauerte Brüstung.
7, 8. Blick vom Kaminplatz in die Sitzgrube (Bild
7) und Gegenblick. Der Wohnbereich wurde weitgehend von Möbeln freigehalten, um den Raumfluß optisch möglichst nicht zu unterbrechen.
Der benötigte Schrankraum ist eingebaut. Die
Unterteilung des großen Fensters nimmt die
Raumgliederung auf: Die Höhe des Oberlicht-
bandes entspricht dem Abstand vom Handlauf
der Galeriebrüstung zur Decke.

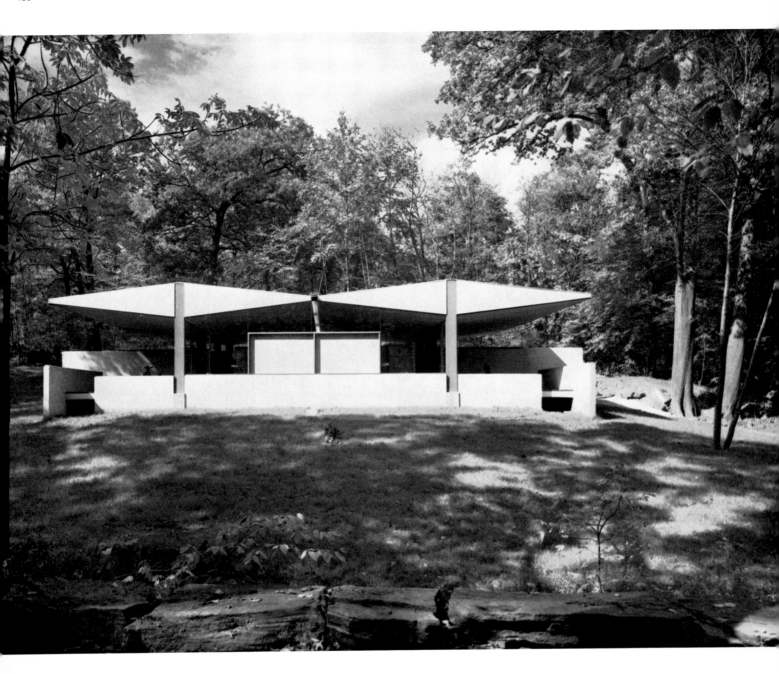

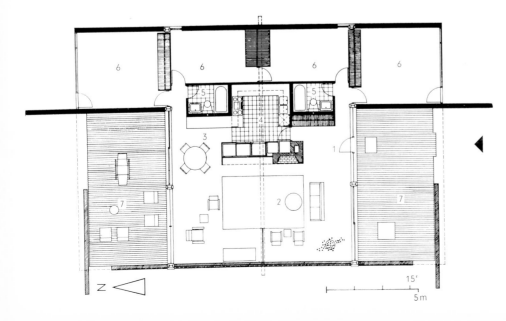

1. East side. The house is entered from the north terrace on the right which leads directly to the living room. The sweep of the roof is recognizable from all sides, as the partitions do not go up to the ceiling. The walls provide obvious contrasts to the floating roof units which are separated from each other by a strip of glazing.

2. Plan. Key: 1 entrance area with cloakroom, 2 living room with sitting area, 3 dining area, 4 kitchen, 5 bathroom and W.C., 6 bedroom, 7 terrace.

3. Towards west, the bedrooms are screened by a brick wall. The shape of the top windows is governed by the sweep of the roof.

4. The view at night conveys a particularly strong impression of the clarity and logic of the structure, with its system of partitions of different heights covered by the floating roof shells.

1. Ostansicht. Der Zugang ins Haus erfolgt von rechts über die Nordterrasse direkt in den Wohnraum. Linie und Bewegung des Daches sind von überall her sichtbar, da die Trennwände nicht bis zur Decke reichen. Die Mauern setzen deutliche Kontraste zu den schwebenden Dachflügeln, die ein Oberlichtband voneinander trennt.

2. Grundriß. Legende: 1 Eingangsbereich mit Garderobe, 2 Wohnbereich mit Sitzgruppe, 3 Eßplatz, 4 Küche, 5 Bad und WC, 6 Schlafraum, 7 Terrasse.

3. Die Schlafräume sind gegen Westen durch eine Ziegelmauer geschlossen. Das Fensterband darüber folgt der Dachlinie.

4. Die Nachtaufnahme macht die Klarheit und Logik der Konstruktion mit ihrem System in der Höhe gestaffelter Mauern und den darüber schwebenden Dachschalen besonders deutlich.

Architect's house at Westchester County, New York
Architect: Ulrich Franzen

In designing his own house, the architect was moved by the intention of creating, for his family, a 'platform for living', covered by two roof shells symbolizing the idea of shelter. The general design of the roof clearly reflects the rationality of modern technology. But at the same time, it is also a symbol for the unity of the family sheltering under it. The platform is sub-divided, as well as separated from the surrounding woods, by a system of partitions of different heights which are nowhere taken right up to the ceiling. The rooms are grouped around a core consisting of two bathrooms and a kitchen. Behind the core on the west side are four bedrooms, placed side by side. The living room, occupying the east side, is separated from the kitchen by a free-standing group of cupboard units which are linked with the open fireplace; it is glazed on three sides and extends into large covered terraces on the north and south sides. Construction: the foundation, consisting of concrete blocks, carries a light steel frame whose posts merely carry the roof. Bolted to the eight posts are triangular lattice beams which carry the I-profile roof rafters. Boarded ceilings; inlaid strip floor. Most of the partitions are free-standing brick walls or glass panels.

Architektenhaus in Westchester County, New York
Architekt: Ulrich Franzen

Beim Entwurf des eigenen Hauses ging der Architekt von dem Grundgedanken aus, für seine Familie eine bewohnbare Plattform zu schaffen und darüber als Schirm zwei gefaltete Dachschalen zu spannen. Die Großstruktur des Daches bringt einerseits die Rationalität des Technologischen klar zum Ausdruck; sie ist zugleich aber auch ein Sinnbild für die Einheit der Familie, die unter diesem Dach lebt. Ein System von unterschiedlich hohen Mauern, die jedoch in keinem Fall bis zur Decke reichen, gliedert die Plattform und grenzt sie gegen den rings umgebenden Wald ab. Die Räume des Hauses gruppieren sich um einen Naßkern, der aus zwei Bädern mit dazwischengeschobener Küche besteht. Hinter dieser Naßzelle sind im Westteil vier Schlafräume nebeneinander aufgereiht. Der Wohnraum im Ostteil wird zur Küche hin durch einen frei stehenden Block aus Schrankelementen abgegrenzt, in den auch der offene Kamin einbezogen ist. Nach Norden und Süden schließt sich an den dreiseitig verglasten Wohnraum jeweils eine große überdachte Terrasse an. Konstruktion: Das aus Zementblocksteinen gemauerte Fundament trägt einen Leichtstahlrahmen, dessen Ständer lediglich das Dach zu tragen haben. An die acht Stützen sind dreieckige Gitterträger geschraubt, die die I-Profile der Dachsparren aufnehmen. Decke holzverschalt. Böden mit Holzriemen belegt. Wände meist als frei stehende Scheiben gemauert oder frei stehende Panels und Glas.

5. South terrace. The parapets are formed by free-standing brick walls of different heights. The glass partition towards the living room consists partly of fixed glazing panels, partly of sliding doors. The under-side of the roof is boarded.

6. The sitting area in the living room is adjacent to the open fireplace which is grouped with the cupboard unit. In the background is the dining area, adjacent to the north terrace. The roof shells do not touch.

5. Blick auf die Südterrasse. Frei stehende Ziegelmauern unterschiedlicher Höhe dienen als Brüstung. Die Glaswände zum Wohnraum sind teils fest verglast, teils als Schiebetüren ausgebildet. Dachunterseite mit Holzriemen verschalt.

6. Die Sitzgruppe des Wohnraums ist dem offenen Kamin zugeordnet, der in das Schrankelement einbezogen ist. Im Hintergrund Eßplatz mit anschließender Nordterrasse. Die Dachschalen stoßen nicht zusammen.

7. The large glazed panels forming the east front are inserted, without frames, between parapet and ceiling. The only steel frame is that of the sliding door leading to the terrace.

8. View through the living room from the north terrace towards the south terrace. A wall panel along the facade and one at right angles to it serve to provide hanging space for pictures and to subdivide the room.

9. One of the bedrooms. The strip window goes round the corner without metal framing.

7. Die großen Glasflächen der Ostseite sind zwischen Brüstung und Decke verspannt. Nur die Schiebetür zur Terrasse hat einen Stahlrahmen.

8. Durchblick von der Nord- zur Südterrasse Eine in der Fassade stehende und eine senkrecht dazu angeordnete Wandscheibe geben Wandfläche für Bilder und gliedern den Raum.

9. Der Schlafraum mit dem sprossenlos übereck geführten Fensterband.

House for H. Taylor at Westport, Connecticut
Architect: John M. Johansen

The flat, park-like site at the Long Island Sound is surrounded by water on three sides – east, west and south. It offers no protection against the hurricanes coming in from the Atlantic so that the desire to protect the house against the elements played a greater part than usual. All the rooms are inserted into a system of curved and intersecting vertical concrete elements which the architect likens to sea shells. The shape and position of these shells are determined by the 'organism' which they enclose and are governed by its functions. This is apparent even from outside inasmuch as the wall units are combined in groups and rise higher near the centre of the house. The innermost group of shells protects the 'heart': the fireside lounge, which is overtowered by the library. Another group comprises the master bedroom, dressing room, study and bathroom; a third group is formed by the utility rooms, kitchen, maid's room and garage. Connecting these groups are the areas planned for general use: living room, dining room and entrance hall. The design of the separate guest house on the north side is governed by the same principles; here, the concrete shells form two apartments. Construction: Load-bearing walls of concrete, rendered or papered on the inside but left untreated on the outside. Ceilings plastered; floors of teak or cork except for the stone flags in the fireside lounge.

Haus H. Taylor in Westport, Connecticut
Architekt: John M. Johansen

Das ebene, parkartige Grundstück am Long Island Sound ist auf drei Seiten – Osten, Westen und Süden – von Wasser umgeben. Es bietet keinerlei Schutz gegen die vom Atlantik kommenden Hurrikans. So rückte der Gedanke, daß ein Haus in erster Linie gegen die Elemente schützen müsse, hier mehr als üblich in den Vordergrund. Alle Räume sind in ein System ineinandergreifender, senkrecht stehender Betonelemente eingefügt, die der Architekt mit den Schalen einer Muschel vergleicht. Form und Stellung dieser Muschelschalen ist durch den »Organismus«, den sie umschließen, bestimmt und folgt dem funktionalen Ablauf des Wohnens. Dieser wird schon von außen sichtbar gemacht, indem die Mauerelemente zu Gruppen zusammengefaßt sind und in ihrer Höhe zum Mittelpunkt des Hauses hin ansteigen. Die innerste Schalengruppe umschließt das »Herz«: das Kaminzimmer, über dem im Turm die Bibliothek liegt. Eine weitere Gruppe umfaßt Schlafraum, Ankleide, Studio und Bad und eine dritte die Wirtschaftsräume mit Küche, Mädchenzimmer und Garage. Bindeglied zwischen diesen Raumgruppen sind die dem allgemeinen Gebrauch dienenden Zonen: Wohnraum, Eßzimmer und Eingangshalle. Konstruktion: Tragende Betonwände, innen verputzt oder tapeziert, außen schalungsroh belassen. Decken verputzt, Böden Teak und Korkeiche, im Kaminzimmer Natursteinplatten.

1. View from the south. This house, built for a physician and his wife, conveys from a distance the impression of a large sculpture, composed of high wall shells curved at the ends. In the centre is the full-height window of the living room, in front of it the outdoor fireplace. Above the living room is the window of the library, on the extreme right the rear wall of the garage.
2. Access road and entrance zone are on the north side where the house has few doors or windows. On the right is the separate guest house.
3. A view of the terrace outside the living room. The open plan with its irregular arrangement of groups of rooms and wall shells provides several sheltered outdoor sitting areas. Because of the risk of flooding, the ground floor is raised about three feet above the ground.

1. Blick von Süden. Dieses Haus für ein Arztehepaar sieht von weitem wie eine Großplastik aus, die aus verschieden hohen, an den Enden abgebogenen Mauerscheiben zusammengesetzt ist. In der Mitte das wandhohe Fenster des Wohnraums, davor der Außenkamin. Über dem Wohnraum das Fenster der Bibliothek. Ganz rechts die Garagenrückwand.
2. Zufahrt und Eingangsbereich auf der Nordseite, die weitgehend geschlossen ist. Rechts das für sich stehende Gästehaus.
3. Blick auf die Terrasse vor dem Wohnraum. Der offene Grundriß mit seinem Ausgreifen von Raumgruppen und Mauerscheiben ergibt mehrere geschützte Freisitzplätze. Das Erdgeschoß ist wegen der Überflutungsgefahr etwa drei Fuß über Terrain angehoben.

4

5

4. This roof view shows particularly clearly the interweaving of the shell-shaped wall units, creating a variegated roof landscape with roofs on different levels.

5. Tower room with library. A few steps lead up to the sundeck at window-sill level.

6. Section and plans of ground floor (left), upper floor (centre) and tower level (right). Key: 1 entrance hall, 2 fireside lounge, 3 living room, 4 terrace, 5 bedroom, 6 study, 7 dressing room, 8 bathroom, 9 dining room, 10 kitchen, 11 maid's room, 12 garage, 13 guest room, 14 library.

7. A view of the dining room; the outdoor sitting area is protected on three sides.

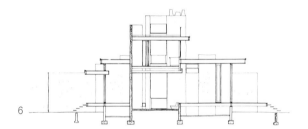

6

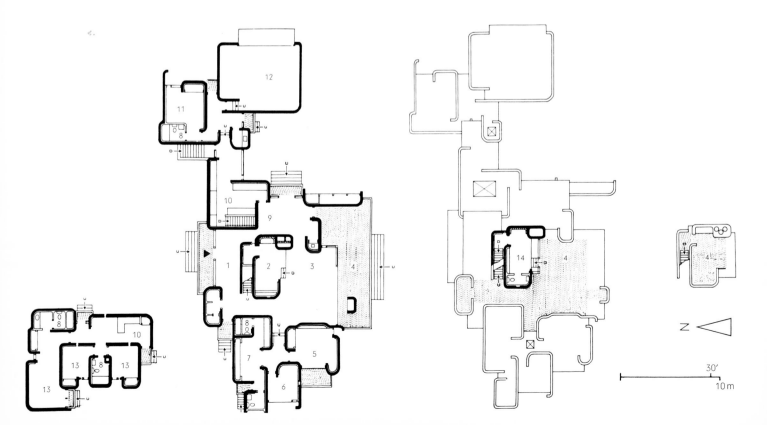

30'

10 m

7

8

8. Living room, with the dining room in the background. Some of the rooms merge and are without doors. The coarse structure of the untreated concrete is emphasized by the smooth plastered ceilings. The shuttering consisted of rough cut, random width oak boarding with rough vertical striation. In all rooms, the ceiling surfaces are separated from the walls by a black plastic strip.
9. From the living room, two steps lead down to the centre of the house which is formed by the fireside lounge. Floor of natural stone flags; fireplace cowl of dark marble.

4. In der Dachaufsicht wird das Ineinandergreifen der schalenförmigen Mauerelemente besonders deutlich. Es entsteht eine bewegte Dachlandschaft mit Dachebenen auf verschiedenen Höhen.
5. Blick in das Turmzimmer mit der Bibliothek. Das in Höhe der Fensterbrüstung liegende Deck erreicht man über eine kleine Treppe.
6. Schnitt und Grundrisse von Erdgeschoß (links), Obergeschoß (Mitte) und Turmplattform (rechts). Legende: 1 Eingangshalle, 2 Kaminzimmer, 3 Wohnraum, 4 Terrasse, 5 Schlafraum, 6 Studio, 7 Ankleide, 8 Bad, 9 Eßzimmer, 10 Küche, 11 Mädchenzimmer, 12 Garage, 13 Gastzimmer, 14 Turmzimmer und Bibliothek.
7. Blick in das Eßzimmer, an das sich ein dreiseitig umschlossener Freisitzplatz anschließt.
8. Wohnraum, dahinter das Eßzimmer. Die Räume gehen zum Teil türenlos ineinander über. Die grobe Struktur des schalungsroh belassenen Betons wird durch die glatten Deckenflächen noch betont. Als Schalungsmaterial sind Eichenbretter verschiedener Breite verwendet, die mit einer extrem groben Säge zugeschnitten und so verlegt wurden, daß unterschiedlich breite Fugen entstanden. Die Deckenfelder sind in allen Räumen durch schwarze Plastikstreifen von den Wänden abgesetzt.
9. Aus dem Wohnraum führen zwei Stufen hinab zur Mitte des Hauses, dem Kaminzimmer. Bodenbelag Natursteinplatten, Kaminschurz aus dunklem Marmor.

9

Photo Credits · Fotonachweis

Th. Andresen, København 36 (1), 38 (4–7), 39 (8–10)

Morley Baer, Berkeley, Cal. 128 (1), 129 (3), 130 (4, 5), 131 (6, 7), 132 (8–10), 133 (11, 12)

Guido Bagutti, Lugano-Massagno 28 (1, 2), 29 (3), 31 (6-9)

Cunvor Betting, København 10 (13), 20 (1), 21 (3), 23 (8–10)

Brecht-Einzig, London 11 (15, 16), 50 (1, 2), 51 (3), 52 (4, 5), 53 (7–9), 54 (10–13), 55 (14–17), 92 (4), 93 (7)

de Burgh Galwey 56 (1, 2), 57 (3, 4), 58 (5, 7), 59 (8–10)

Robert Damora, Bedford Village, N. Y. 162 (1, 2), 163 (3), 164 (4, 5), 165 (7–9)

Domus 44 (1), 45 (2), 46 (4), 47 (7), 48 (9, 11, 12), 49 (13, 14)

Max Dupain, Sydney 110 (1), 111 (3), 112 (4–7), 113 (9)

Max Dupain – Kerry Durdas, Sydney 11 (14), 40 (1), 41 (2), 42 (3), 43 (5–8)

Alexandre Georges, New City, N. Y. 9 (10), 114 (1), 116 (3, 4), 117 (5, 6), 118 (8–10), 119 (11–13)

K. Helmer-Petersen, København 7 (3), 12 (1, 2), 13 (5), 14 (6, 7), 15 (8, 9), 23 (6, 7)

Sam Lambert, London 6 (1), 94 (1), 95 (2, 3), 96 (6), 97 (7–9), 98 (10, 11), 99 (12, 13)

Joseph W. Molitor, Ossining, N.Y. 154 (1), 156 (5, 6), 157 (7, 8)

Horstheinz Neuendorff, Baden-Baden 68 (1), 69 (2), 70 (3, 4), 71 (6–8), 72 (9, 10), 73 (11–13), 100 (1), 102 (4, 5), 103 (6, 7), 104 (8, 9), 105 (10–12)

Thomas Pedersen & Poul Pedersen, Århus 74 (1, 3), 75 (4), 76 (5–7), 77 (9, 10)

Marvin Rand, Los Angeles, Cal. 7 (4), 64 (1), 65 (3), 66 (4–7), 67 (8)

Simo Rista 134 (1, 2), 137 (6, 7), 138 (8–10), 139 (11, 12)

Ben Schnall, Hewlett Harbor, N.Y. 124 (1), 125 (3), 126 (4–7), 127 (8, 9)

Julius Shulman, Los Angeles, Cal. 8 (7), 32 (1), 33 (3), 34 (4–6), 35 (7–10), 120 (1), 121 (2), 122 (3, 4), 123 (6–9), 148 (1), 149 (2, 3), 151 (6, 7), 152 (8–10), 153 (11–14)

Douglas M. Simmonds, Los Angeles, Cal. 140 (1), 141 (3, 4), 142 (5, 6), 143 (7–9)

Henk Snoek, London 90 (1, 2), 91 (3), 93 (6, 8)

Ezra Stoller Associates, Mamaroneck, N.Y. 10 (12), 16 (1), 17 (4), 18 (5–7), 19 (8–10), 158 (1), 159 (3, 4), 160 (5, 6), 161 (7–9)

Strüwing, København 8 (6), 24 (1, 2), 25 (4, 5), 26 (6, 7), 27 (8–10), 60 (1), 61 (3), 62 (5, 6), 63 (7–9), 106 (1, 2), 108 (4, 5), 109 (7, 8, 10)

Else Tholstrup 78 (1), 79 (3, 4), 80 (5–7), 81 (9,10), 82 (11–13), 83 (14, 15)

Albert Winkler, Bern 6 (2), 84 (1, 2), 85 (4), 86 (5), 87 (7–10), 88 (11, 12), 89 (13–15)